film appreciation

film
appreciation

Allan Casebier

University of Southern California

Harcourt Brace Jovanovich, Inc.

New York   Chicago   San Francisco   Atlanta

ISBN: 0-15-527370-1

Library of Congress Catalog Card Number: 75-43150

Printed in the United States of America

preface

The motion picture as an art form is a relatively recent development. Because it is so new, it is difficult to gain a firm grasp of its nature, although many theories of film have been advanced during its brief history. While helpful on the whole, these theories have tended to deal with film in terms of other arts. Those coming to a study of film with a background in drama emphasize its commonalities with the theatre—acting, dialogue, *mise en scène;* historians of art see the film image largely in terms of balance, proportion, rhythm, volume, textures; and literary critics apply to films the linguistic and symbolic systems of interpretation they use in analysis of fiction and poetry.

Over and above these connections with other art forms, film is a particular result of wedding the traditional elements of actor, setting, dialogue, costume, and music to the new possibilities generated by the camera and the editing process. This book aims to illuminate that result. Part I deals with the basic matter of film—the visual and aural elements and those cinematic devices dependent on an audience's perceptual and emotional capacities. Part 2 focuses on how the film image creates reality—and unreality. Part 3 closes the book with an examination of cinematic styles and of some theoretical bases of film criticism.

A full appreciation of motion pictures requires familiarity with the aesthetic dimensions of films, and the emphasis here will accordingly be on identifying the qualities involved and on understanding the visual, aural, and other aspects of a movie that bring those qualities into being. However, because the aesthetic effect of a given visual or aural element is determined partly by the other elements with which it interacts, evaluation of any *one* of those elements by itself (camera movement, type of set, particular optical effect, or whatever) can never be without qualification. At best, one can say only that a given element *tends* to produce a certain effect.

Many scenes and sequences from various motion pictures are cited and described throughout the book. Description inevitably requires interpretation, and, because films (as all works of art) invite differing interpretations, I wish to emphasize that those presented here are offered only as *some* useful ways of regarding the films discussed.

Thanks are due Toho Films Inc., Contemporary/McGraw-Hill Films, Inc., and The Pacific Film Archive for permitting me to study films discussed in this book. I wish to thank colleagues Irwin Blacker, Arthur Knight, Marsha Kinder, Donald Staples, Alexander Sesonske, and Gene Coe for helpful discussion and suggestions. One of my students, Joe Saunders, also made many useful suggestions and helped in preparing stills for the book. Most of all, I want to thank my wife, Janet, whose editing of the manuscript made this book possible.

Allan Casebier

contents

9 critical interpretation 153

10 evaluating films 173

film appreciation

the
film
medium

PART
ONE

PART
ONE

PART
ONE

PA
ON

The visual qualities of a film are composed of several factors—film stock, lenses, shooting angle, camera position, framing, camera and object movement, editing, optics, and *mise en scène.*

One might regard these factors as of interest to filmmakers but not to appreciators of the motion picture. The fact is, however, that all visual qualities are perceivable by moviegoers who make the effort to see them. Once recognized, they can become a source for much of the pleasure to be derived from movies. In some films—where the action is indicated by only one or two visual elements—their recognition is crucial for understanding.

visual
elements

Film Stock

Grain and Contrast

The type of film used in photographing a subject has much to do with the artistic quality of the finished product. The two features of film stock that have the greatest influence upon the look of a motion picture are *grain* and *contrast*. Grain refers to the size of the particles that make up the film image. Coarse-grain film produces a "grainy" image, and fine-grain film, a smoother one. Contrast refers to the differentiation in gradations of intensity, or *tone*, that the film is capable of recording.

In *The Battle of Algiers* (1967) the director, Gillo Pontecorvo, shot the street scenes with film that gave a grainy image. This look was effective in two ways. First, since documentary-newsreel footage is often shot with such film, it gave *The Battle of Algiers* a look of on-the-spot filming of actual events.

The Battle of Algiers, *1967*

In fact, the look was so convincing that it was necessary to announce at the beginning of the film that all its events were staged. Second, the graininess gave a desired harshness to the views of Algiers, which otherwise would have been altogether too soft and pretty for a drama of such a harsh, brutal nature.

By contrast, Bo Widerberg's *Elvira Madigan* (1967) was shot with a fine-grain film, which gave a smooth loveliness that enhanced its romantic mood and atmosphere.

Other films combine the two types of film stock. In Ingmar Bergman's *Wild Strawberries* (1957), for example, the nightmares of the central character are shot with a grainy stock and the scenes of lyrical remembrance with a smooth, nongrainy stock.

With respect to the differentiation capability of film stock (described above), in black-and-white film there is a great range possible. In John Ford's *The Informer* (1935) the beauty and variety of fog was brought out by the film stock, which exhibited a large number of differentiations on the gray scale, ranging from near white to near black. A film stock with a more limited range of gray differentiations would have recorded the various forms of fog shown as looking very much the same.

In some contexts, a film stock with high contrast is desirable—as, for example, where stark contrasts between black and white are expressive of a polarized situation. The nightmare that opens Bergman's *Wild Strawberries* is typical of this use of film stock.

In color film the discernible values of a hue are tantamount to the gradations of gray in black-and-white film. Stanley Donen's *Two for the Road* (1967) indicated place and time in many scenes by subtle differences in costume and locale conveyed by differences in color.

Color and Black and White

In addition to choices made with regard to the grain and tonal differentiations of various film stocks, filmmakers must decide whether to use *black-and-white* or *color* film stock.

As has often been emphasized, neither black and white nor color is intrinsically better artistically. Each has its own expressive potentials. The following qualities of color are those among which the filmmaker must choose according to the effects aimed for with respect to theme, character, action, and setting. Differences in *value* (shades of a color) are usually more easily perceived in color. This feature helps to convey a theme visually rather than through dialogue or narration (devices that are often too obvious). In his *Muriel* (1963) Alain Resnais makes use of the greater variations in shades provided by color to express the idea that the past cannot be recaptured. Sequences in which characters recall relationships and events are shot largely in pale, grayed colors rather than pure ones. Blue-grays and beiges mark the unclear and indistinct status of memory images, and the fragmentation of memory is conveyed by mixing colors in a jumble—similar to the random slipping in and out of consciousness of our own everyday experience of memories.

When color's greater detail is combined with the vividness of which color is capable, another effect results. Color scenes frequently seem closer in time and space than black-and-white scenes. Another Alain Resnais film, *Night and Fog* (1955), draws upon this difference to make convincing its central theme that we cannot fully know the past. In this documentary of World War II Nazi concentration camps, black-and-white newsreel and still photos taken at the time of the camps' operation are set against color photography of the remnants of the camps in the present, emphasizing the sense of distance and remoteness from the past.

In exterior shots, color generally conveys a sense of space more easily than black and white. Given that blue tends to "recede" while a color such as red "advances," careful arrangement of action, with advancing colors in the foreground and receding colors in the background, increases the feeling of spaciousness in a film. Some of the beauty of the great outdoors that marked a western like George Stevens' *Shane* (1953) can be traced to the use of this expressive potential of color.

Color generally permits a greater range of contrasts than black and white. Color is often better at amplifying mood and is more successful at bringing out differences between certain features of a film's reality. *Fellini's Satyricon* (1969) draws upon these capacities of color film in its attempt to rid us of a myth about the ancient world. Antiquity, the subject of the film, has often been thought of as "a serene, classical, statuesque, clean world."[1] The film provides quite a different portrayal. Nothing in the world of this film is luminous, white, or shining. During most of the film one experiences darkness, night, and the shadowy. "Clothes are dingy, in opaque colors with the qualities of stone and dust."[2] Scenes of luxury are in clouded blacks, reds, yellows, and browns. In a highlight of the film, Trimalchio's feast, the faces of the privileged class look unreal (red, blue, green casts), and bizarre dress and coiffures are accented with rich reddish oranges, while the food is predominantly brown. By contrast, the poor guests at the feast are placed in areas marked by unextravagant and neutral colors such as black and gray. The viewer is struck by the fact that in antiquity, decadence, extravagance, and unreality existed side by side with the commonplace.

A crucial factor in the aesthetic uses of cinematic color is time.[3] In film, the order and duration of color images must be attended to with great care. A color shown too long loses its force; one shown for too short a time can fail in its impact. In Alfred Hitchcock's *Vertigo* (1958) a specific color progression is used. In the early parts, exteriors tend toward greens and blues and interiors toward browns, oranges, and yellows. Toward the end, when Scotty (Jimmy Stewart) has turned Judy into Madeline (both played by Kim Novak) in a wish-fulfillment illusion, the color scheme reverses, indicating the transformation of Stewart's perception of the world.[4] He embraces Judy in a scene illuminated by a green neon sign that alters interiors to a color that had marked exteriors earlier.

Though the motivation for this alteration in color scheme is to portray an illusion, the scenes are realistic in isolation. It is only in sequence that they help create the fantasy.

There is of course no reason why objects in a film must have the colors they have in nature. The director Carl Dreyer foresees films in which sky would be green, grass blue, and oceans red, all the elements being woven together to give an impressionistic texture.[5]

Positive or Negative

Another choice open to a filmmaker in selecting stock is whether to produce positive or negative (light and dark reversed) images. In black and white, *positive image* is by far the most common, being used for virtually every film

[1] Alberto Moravia and Federico Fellini, "Documentary of a Dream: A Dialogue Between Alberto Moravia and Federico Fellini." In *Fellini's Satyricon,* ed. by Dario Zanelli (New York: Ballantine Books, 1969), p. 27.
[2] Ibid., p. 28.
[3] For a discussion of this concept, see Rudolf Arnheim, *Art and Visual Perception* (Berkeley: University of California Press, 1954), p. 363.
[4] William Johnson, "Coming to Terms with Color." In *The Movies as Medium,* Lewis Jacobs (New York: Farrar, Straus & Giroux, 1970), p. 236.
[5] Carl Dryer, "Color and Color Films." In *Movies as Medium,* Jacobs, p. 198.

one sees. *Negative image* is an effect that must be used with restraint because of its emphatic character.

Negative image confers, among other things, a quality of unreality. In his *Alphaville* (1965) Jean-Luc Godard emphasizes the unreal qualities of a future civilization by suddenly throwing a chase scene into negative image. F. W. Murnau, in his recounting of the Dracula story in *Nosferatu* (1922), films the hero's arrival in negative image. Since the look of negative image is akin to that of an X-ray film, the scene evokes associations of the macabre, the actor looking like a skeleton and the world seemingly drained of life.

Negative image in color produces not the reversal of black and white, but an orange and blue-green world, with an overall look that is most unpleasing. There can be, no doubt, artistic motivations for the use of this effect. Someone like Andy Warhol may well use negative color stock at some time in the future to shock an audience and blunt its senses.

Use of Filters

Both color and black-and-white filming can be enhanced by the use of filters. Some filters are designed strictly for use in conjunction with one or the other film stock, but there are also all-purpose filters that are effective with either color or black and white. Filters can alter all or only part of the look and quality of an image depending on what the specific artistic context requires. Their function is to compensate for the fact that unfiltered tones often do not match what the unaided human eye sees or to alter the look of things for some expressionistic purpose.

Besides altering colors, filters can bring out tonal gradations in black-and-white film. (Black-and-white film stock tends to be insensitive to the tonal gradations of greens in nature or to differentiations between cloud and sky.)

Some artistic contexts (for example, a darkened sky symbolizing an impending event) demand that only part of an image be altered. An all-purpose filter called a *polarizing filter* provides a way of darkening the sky while retaining the color values of other aspects of the environment.

There are other uses of filters: to improve appearance by softening the image (the *diffusion filter*); to create fog and haze effects *(Harrison fog filters);* and to create low contrast and reduce color saturation *(Harrison low-contrast screens).* In the reunion scene in Arthur Penn's *Bonnie and Clyde* (1967) the hero and heroine have escaped from a hectic nationwide manhunt. A red filter lends a pervasive hazy, pastel look to the warm, slow-paced, low-keyed meeting with Bonnie's mother, conveying the nostalgic warmth that Bonnie and her mother feel for one another.

Lenses

The type of lens used in shooting has an extremely important effect on what we see. Lenses include fish-eye, wide-angle, normal, long (including the often used telephoto), and zoom. Lenses are often manipulated to produce a soft-focus image.

A *fish-eye lens* gives such a flagrantly unreal appearance to things that its use must be restricted to special circumstances where the intent is to communicate a bizarre situation or distorted viewpoint.

A *wide-angle lens* can be used in large portions of films for expressive purposes. Claude Chabrol's *The Cousins* (1958) provides a fascinating example of how wide-angle lenses can be used for artistic effect. The space we live in every day has sharp, well-defined lines. Door frames have a straight up-and-down rectangularity, and they maintain these lines as we move through them. Walls, windows, picture frames, chairs, and tables have a similar character. The wide-angle lenses used in *The Cousins* break down these solid lines. As Chabrol's camera moves through the photographed space, objects distort, lines become wavy, and the spatial reality as a whole becomes fluid in appearance. The result is that the environment portrayed in the film lacks the rigid, solid, dependable character that we associate with everyday spaces. When at the end of the film a horrifying event occurs, the nature of the film's space supports the action. The audience can accept the horrifying event partly because it has been perceiving an undependable environment in which it is not surprising when something out of the ordinary happens.

The *normal lens* (the one most like that of the eye) is suited to capturing the rigid lines and solidity of everyday environments. This lens provides the kind of spatial appearance that Chabrol wanted to break down. Vittorio De Sica used a normal lens in his neorealist drama *Bicycle Thief* (1947) to create the naturalistic environment of the film.

The *telephoto lens,* which is the longest of the long lenses, has a capacity to compress the visual field—thus giving it a distorted appearance. In a rather striking shot near the beginning of Mike Nichols' *Catch 22* (1969), military aircraft preparing for a flight are seen via a telephoto lens. As they taxi to the takeoff area, the compression produced by the lens gives them a bizarre, stubby appearance that fits with and foreshadows the portrayal of the absurd which follows. In another Nichols film, *The Graduate* (1967), a telephoto-lens shot shows Dustin Hoffman running through the streets of Santa Barbara on his way to prevent the marriage of the girl he loves to another man. The distortion of Hoffman's movements gives us the feeling that he is running hard but getting nowhere—an impression that is expressive of what is happening at that point in the story.

Although *zoom lenses* do not generally render as sharp an image as the lenses of fixed focal length discussed above, they have advantages that have led to their rather frequent use in recent years. These lenses, which have a rapidly variable focal length, can give the appearance of moving the camera closer to (or farther from) the subject. A problem with zooming is that three-dimensional perspective becomes somewhat distorted. Space looks flat or two-dimensional when compared to a shot of the same subject taken by a camera that is closer to it. In the case of the latter, as the camera moves

Bicycle Thief, *1947*

forward objects pass by on either side, giving a feeling of depth. In the case of the former, camera-to-subject distance remains the same and the sensation of depth is sacrificed. An advantage of zooming is that it can very forcefully direct audience attention to a subject. This channeling of vision can highlight just the part of a situation that needs to be recognized. Moreover, in filming documentaries, the zoom is an effective tool for getting a close-up view of people without making them overly conscious of the camera's presence.

Lenses can also affect the appearance of images through focusing: *sharp focus* gives an appearance that conforms more closely to the everyday look of things; *soft focus* blurs and softens shapes. Soft focus has been used to create an aura of romance, to establish an atmosphere of mystery, to express a character's feelings (fainting, delirium), or to focus attention on one part of the screen.

Shooting Angle

The angle from which an action, event, or character is shot varies enormously with the artistic intent involved. Orson Welles photographed many sequences in *Citizen Kane* (1940) upward from a low angle against an enclosed space. This shooting direction gave a feeling of containment to the action. On the other hand, in every Hitchcock film a startling effect is produced by his trademark shot, in which the camera peers straight down from a great height. Perhaps the most memorable of these shots is the one in *Vertigo* in which Jimmy Stewart gazes down from the dizzying heights of a bell tower.

Citizen Kane, *1940*

The Third Man, *1949*

The standard shooting angle has, however, been one that approximates our everyday view of things. *Shane* was shot in this "normal" style.

Sir Carol Reed's *The Third Man* (1949), on the other hand, uses many unusual, tilted camera angles, which distort the appearance of the characters, objects, and events of the environment, to highlight the dramatic, sinister, and bizarre nature of the film.

Another function of shooting angle is the presentation of varying viewpoints. Many films provide only an outsider's viewpoint, with the camera (and hence the viewer) an unseen eavesdropper on the action. When character viewpoint is used, we see how the world looks to someone according to his or her state of consciousness or mood (happy, sad, alienated, drunk, delirious). For example, when a character has lost interest in some person or object, his or her feelings may be vividly represented by a character-viewpoint shot in which that person or object appears in soft focus while other elements within view are in sharp focus. A superhuman viewpoint may also be used. This occurs when the shooting angle provides a viewpoint that no human perceiver could possibly have. The opening shot from Orson Welles' *Touch of Evil* (1957), discussed in Chapter 2, is an excellent example of this viewpoint.

Camera Position

Camera positions during a shot may range from close-up to long, with a medium distance again providing a kind of "normal" perspective. Bergman's *Cries and Whispers* (1972) is agonizing in content and slow-moving in pace. It is shot in such extreme close-ups that its especially excruciating moments force themselves almost unbearably on the viewer.

One of the best artistic uses of the long shot occurs in Chaplin's *The Gold Rush* (1925) in the scene where a group of people ascend a hillside. The effect of the long perspective is to turn their movement into a composition of motion on a landscape.

As in the case of shooting angle, there is a "normal" distance for camera position that gives a relatively full view of a character. From this distance, we are neither too far away to see the salient features nor so close as to be distracted by the slightest movement of an eyebrow. The Bogart thrillers of the 1940s and 1950s, made under the guidance of Howard Hawks and John Huston, dwelled upon this middle distance. The effect was that camera position did not obtrude into the audience's awareness of the action.

The Gold Rush, *1925*

Framing

First and foremost among the artistic uses of framing is the fact that its presence establishes a *screen space.* Events occurring within this space have a significance that events in an unbounded space do not have. For instance, the convergence of characters' movements on the screen tends to indicate that something important is going to happen. In our everyday living space, with its lack of a frame, similar movements of people toward one another would carry no such implication.

Within screen space the relative size *(scale)* of persons and objects also assumes prominence. Roman Polanski's *Knife in the Water* (1962) provides an especially graphic illustration of how scale can be used to develop dramatic relationships. The story centers around three people: a married couple and a boy whom they meet by chance on their way to a weekend outing aboard their boat.

Early in the film the man is seen in an extreme close-up, with the boy in the background. In this shot and many others that follow, scale is expressive of the relationships between them. The close-up view of the man makes him dominate the screen space. His relative hugeness contrasts with the tiny image size accorded the boy. The man's dominance of the boy is thereby expressed via scale. Once aboard the boat, however, the scale and thematic relations are reversed. Now the boy commands attention in the foreground while the man is seen as a relatively small figure in the background.

In still another shot, the relative positions within the framed screen space are indicative of the situation. Here the boy's location between the couple is expressive of the emotional swath that he has cut through their relationship.

Akira Kurosawa's *Sanjuro* (1962), a samurai film with a flavor much like that of an American western, embodies another example of the use of framing to indicate relationships. Its hero, Sanjuro (played by Toshiro Mifune), becomes the leader of a group of nine sincere but somewhat inept young men. Framing is used to sensitize the audience to Mifune's relationship to the Nine.

The film's interiors are composed of walls with square panels and bold vertical-horizontal patterns, typifying a highly ordered environment. The camera holds its position throughout action that is shot against these interiors, establishing a fixed frame for the characters' postures and movements. The fixed framing and the sets combine to do two things—heighten audience awareness of screen graphics and increase the audience's sense of the humorous relationship between Mifune and the Nine.

For example, an amusing theme is the contrast between the rigid order in which the Nine move and the ineptness of their movements. Whenever they prepare to go out, they form themselves into a straight line. As they move along, they convey the impression of an Asian dragon, with Mifune as the head and the Nine as the body. Throughout the film each of the Nine holds a rigidly vertical posture.

Sanjuro, *1962*

Mifune's posture and screen placement contrast with that of the Nine. Sometimes his dominance is graphically represented by his placement in isolation on one side of the screen, with the Nine grouped together on the other side; at other times he leads them in their deliberations from the center of a circle that they form around him; on still other occasions his large figure dwarfs theirs. His independence from them is portrayed in several shots where his reclining posture, with its flamboyant lines, contrasts with the Nine's linearity.

The Offscreen Image

Framing establishes not only an inside, with the various qualities just surveyed; it also establishes an outside. Many of the powerful effects of cinema have been grounded in the interaction between what is inside and what is outside the frame.

Offscreen images and action can be located in seven places outside the screen area: above, below, to either side of the framed area, too far in the distance to be seen in the framed area, blocked off from sight within the framed area (as, for example, something behind a wall), and behind the camera. The offscreen dimension can work just as powerfully when only parts of objects or parts of characters and their actions are out of view.

The use of offscreen images is evident in well-established cinematic genres. What horror movie could evoke the slightest suspense, fear, tension, or anticipation without being able to place its monsters, ghouls, ghosts, and otherwise mysterious presences out of sight? The space behind the camera has been prominently used in the horror film. Horror films often draw our attention to the area behind the camera by giving the camera itself a distinctive personality. This personality exists whenever the camera seems to be a real perceiver, watching the action of a film while remaining unseen. The eerie atmosphere common to horror films is caused in part by camera personality.

The western is also illustrative of the use of the offscreen image. Imagine an obligatory showdown or shootout sequence without the sudden appearance from off screen of the "bad guy." How tepid chase sequences would be, too, if all actions of pursued and pursuer were on screen. The far-off distance of screen space is an offscreen space commonly found in the western genre. What western would be complete without a scene in which its characters look expectantly off into the distance, awaiting the arrival of the hero or heroine?

To illustrate the indispensability of offscreen space in all films one need only imagine a film without any images placed out of sight. If all action took place within screen space, entrances and exits would have to be planned so that their occurrence would not draw attention from the main onscreen action. A result would be that the audience would forget any characters not on screen. It would seem axiomatic that where the audience has that little involvement with the characters, the story has failed aesthetically. Also, characters in the story would have to be oblivious of other characters when they were off screen, which would severely limit development of the story.

In a memorable scene near the end of Martin Ritt's *Hud* (1963), a cattleman (played by Melvyn Douglas) decides to submit his herd of cattle to a test for hoof-and-mouth disease rather than sell them as Hud (Paul Newman) had urged him. As it turns out, the herd is diseased and must be destroyed. When the animals enter the slaughter area from screen top and innocently descend vertically through screen space, we hear their loud, collective sound. Next Melvyn Douglas' men are shown firing at the animals. Most of the effects of the gunfire upon the animals are off screen, and the carnage that must be taking place is left to the imagination. Treating the killing of the herd as an offscreen event creates tension and increases our involvement in what is taking place.

Sergei Eisenstein's silent film *The Battleship Potemkin* (1925) contains a brilliant sequence (dubbed the "Odessa Steps" sequence) that has been heavily analyzed for its onscreen characteristics, which have a high degree of interesting graphic content. It is important to recognize, however, that offscreen images also play a crucial role in developing the action of the sequence.

The film is about a mutiny (in support of the revolution) aboard the Russian battleship *Potemkin* in 1905. As the ship pulls into the friendly port of Odessa with the mutinous sailors aboard, small boats sail out to escort it in and well-wishers gather on steps that lead into the city from the shore. The crowd on the steps is suddenly attacked by government troops, who force them to retreat down the steps. At the bottom the crowd is attacked by troops on horseback. The cannons of the battleship fire at the troops, but they are too late to save

The Battleship Potemkin, *1925*

most of the well-wishers. The sequence ends with the battleship firing on the headquarters of the Russian generals who ordered the assault.

The opening shots of the sequence provide a pleasant spectacle as the Odessa boats go out to escort the battleship into port. Much action is crowded into the onscreen area, with little to distract our interest and imagination off screen. There is much compositional value in what is happening on screen at this point, and we focus attention on the patterns made by the sailboats, much as one might look at a painting.

After the boats reach the battleship, the orientation of action changes. Where before action had been moving mostly screen right, it now moves directly toward the camera or directly away from it. Sailors arrive on screen from behind the camera; well-wishers on the shore wave toward the camera. The escort boats sail toward the camera. Melons passed from boat to boat to be placed on the battleship come from behind the camera.

This shift in the direction of action makes the audience aware of the off-screen area behind the camera.[6] Now it seems less easy to take the role of onlooker of action occurring apart from oneself. Now it seems as if some of the action comes from inside the movie theater, and this sense of things happening off screen behind the camera heightens audience involvement in the action.

As the action on the steps begins, the orderliness of the screen composition begins to dissipate. The pleasant compositions and distanced attitude that marked the introduction are now replaced by involvement and disorder. The action is fragmented, and sharp lines forming diagonals now mark onscreen images.

As the soldiers advance, we see only partial views of them. We imagine their faces and their intentions as they march mechanically down the steps on their assault. It is the same with the attacked. We are presented with only fragmented shots of their reaction. A woman with a baby is hit by gunfire and, as she falls, sets her baby's carriage in motion. With her baby inside, the carriage runs wild, plummeting down the steps. As it rolls, the viewer feels tension about the fate of the innocent child inside.

At this point, the offscreen action dominates one's consciousness. The audience wonders how many of the people have been shot, what is happening on the battleship, when the ship will counterattack, and how close the advancing troops are—all interests involving offscreen elements.

The main thrust of offscreen movement continues forward toward the viewer. This tends to involve viewers in the action and forces them to imagine what is happening in the offscreen area behind the camera. In the next shot we see the guns of the battleship point directly at the camera as the ship prepares to counterattack. Again the audience must focus its attention on the offscreen area behind the camera.

[6] For analyses of the aesthetic uses of offscreen space, see Joe Saunders, "Off-Screen Images" (Ph.D. diss., University of Southern California, 1975), and Noel Burch, *The Theory of Film Practice* (New York: Praeger, 1973), Chapter 2.

The sequences close with a series of shots that center around the theme of disorder. First the battleship fires into the Odessa Theatre area—the location of the area's military headquarters. Three rapid shots follow of statues of lions—lying, half risen, then fully risen. The statues seem to register their alarm at the violence and disorder that has taken place on the Odessa Steps. The final shot of the sequence leaves us with an image of disorder, as smoke and flying debris fill the screen after the battleship scores a hit on the walls of the headquarters' area.

The effectiveness of an offscreen image derives from the fact that the audience (in its imagination) supplies its location and character. Moreover, what is off screen for one or more shots often becomes on screen in subsequent shots. In this case, we may say that the camera retrospectively reveals what was off screen, as well as revealing its location and characteristics.

To analyze the offscreen effect, therefore, it is not enough to identify what is off screen at any point in a film. We must also examine a vital relationship: that between what the audience imagined to be off screen and what *was*. Some of the most powerful aesthetic effects result from that relationship of audience expectation and the later revelation.

Polanski's *Rosemary's Baby* (1968) is filled with retrospective revelations of this sort. In one scene, Rosemary (played by Mia Farrow) seems endangered by a sinister group of people living in a neighboring apartment. In the shocking final scene, she makes her way into that apartment (off screen to this point) to find a witches' coven celebrating the birth of her baby (whom they take to also be the offspring of the devil). Because it is the culmination of many imagined offscreen events, the scene has great impact.

Rosemary's Baby, *1968*

Retrospective revelations may also be used to show the audience that what it had imagined to be off screen was actually not there. Excruciating tension is created in a horror film when its heroine hears a sound, becomes apprehensive about the presence of some unseen person, and cautiously makes her way toward the possible danger. When the camera finally reveals it to be a cat, the audience breathes a sigh of relief. In many horror movie contexts such a retrospective revelation provides a needed respite from scenes of horror.[7]

Camera and Object Movement

Stationary and Moving Camera

In photographing a subject, one can move the camera or have it remain stationary. The expressive potentials of the stationary camera include *panning* (from *panorama*), where it makes a steady continous movement across an object or space; *tilting,* where it moves up or down to record its subject; and combinations of these movements *(tilt-pan).*

Luis Buñuel's *Tristana* (1970) contains a shot that begins with a pan over the façade of an old building and develops into a tilt down to a young couple in the square below. This pan-tilt contrasts the solid and unconcerned visage of an ancient building with the agitated, volatile state of the young couple.

The moving camera can track forward, backward, left or right in providing its view of the subject. Movements forward or backward through a space give the audience the illusion of moving through the screen space. This sensation of movement gives cinematic space many of the qualities of the space of architecture. The masses of an artistically well-designed building are distributed so that, moving through its space, one has a series of well-coordinated visual experiences.

A camera tracking left or right along a subject has rather different artistic potentials. The flat screen space—like an unrolling band—created by Jean-Luc Godard in films such as *Weekend* (1968), *One Plus One* (or *Sympathy for the Devil,* 1968), *Wind from the East* (1969), and *Tout Va Bien* (1972) was obtained using a left- or right-tracking camera.[8]

The camera mounted on a dolly or some other mobile platform produces a type of camera movement that gives a view of the action that is smooth, so that one's attention is not drawn toward the movement or distracted by it from the action. A moving camera that is hand-held usually gives a shaky, uneven view of the action. The rough or shaky look created by the hand-held camera makes us aware of the action and gives a sense of being there. The image produced

[7] For a discussion of the value of providing audience relief in this film genre, see François Truffaut, *Hitchcock* (New York: Simon and Schuster, 1967), p. 221.
[8] Brian Henderson, "Toward a Non-Bourgeois Camera Style," *Film Quarterly* 24, no. 2 (Winter 1970–71), pp. 2–14.

by a hand-held camera, however, is not naturalistic or realistic when compared to our everyday view of things; our perception ordinarily adjusts as we move, so as to give a smooth view of the world.

One of the many aesthetic effects obtainable with the hand-held camera appears in Bernardo Bertolucci's *The Conformist* (1971). The desperate chase through the woods, which ends in the brutal killing of the character played by Dominique Sanda, is portrayed with the unstable rhythms and appearances usually obtained with the hand-held camera. The chaotic and unstable world thus portrayed is appropriate to the horrifying scene.

Motion in a film is a function of objects in it, as well as of the camera. The animate and inanimate objects that populate a film can, as in life, roll, fall, turn, twist, fly, swim, and otherwise move in varying relationships to the camera.

An instructive comparison of camera and object movement can be made using Shirley Clarke's *Bridges-Go-Round* (1959) and Bruce Baillie's *Castro Street* (1966). Clarke moves her camera to film New York's bridges in a way that gives these stationary objects beauty. Her camera is so active that it almost seems the bridges are moving. By contrast, Baillie uses a stationary camera to pan and tilt over the beauty in the actual motions of objects in a northern California street.

Resnais' *Night and Fog,* discussed above with reference to conveying an impression of the past by alternating color and black and white, uses camera movement to amplify this impression. Still photos of conditions, events, and people, taken while the concentration camps were in use, are juxtaposed against shots of the camps in the present in which the camera is constantly in motion. The effect of this contrast is to make it seem as if the past were frozen, dead, still, and lifeless, while the present seems alive, constantly in flux, and shifting in form.

The implication is that the present is as difficult to grasp as the past. This fluidity of the present connects with what is explicitly stated in the dialogue— that we know the present no better than we know the past: Just as we forget what happened in those concentration camps, so we fail to realize the presence of murderers in our own times and places.

Night and Fog employs a stationary camera to aesthetic advantage as well. The film establishes a rhythm for its panning and tilting to which we become accustomed. A scene well along in the film begins with a typical pan-tilt—this time over a pile of human hair. But the camera alters its rhythm this time, continuing the tilt up and up to reveal that the collected human hair is not, as we had thought, a pile, but rather something more like a mountain. We realize how deceptive a documentary camera style can be, for the rhythm that this scene uses and then breaks with is standard for documenting.

We come to a film with the expectation that a subject such as the concentration camp phenomenon can be "documented." A deeply embedded assumption about our knowledge of the past is challenged by *Night and Fog.* This is that knowledge about a past phenomenon like the Nazi camps has its source in actions such as visiting their remnants and consulting documents such as records, eyewitness reports, and stills and motion pictures made at the time. *Night and Fog* is composed entirely of an exploration of these familiar sources for past knowledge, and the treatment, as in the case of stationary camera examination of documents and remnants, is of standard documentary form. Yet when a receptive audience has experienced the film, it is left with the impression that the full reality of the camps has escaped its view.

Fast and Slow Motion

Motion filmed at a speed greater than the normal 24 frames per second and projected at normal speed will give the effect called *slow motion.* Just the reverse is true for *fast motion.* Slow motion has a capacity to call attention to motion itself, and attention focused on the character of an actor's motion somewhat lessens our interest in what this motion will accomplish.

At the end of *Bonnie and Clyde,* Clyde Barrow's fall as he is riddled with bullets is portrayed in slow motion. His fall looks of greater consequence than it would have had it been filmed at normal speed. The use of slow motion connects with the dominant theme of the movie: that Bonnie and Clyde are mythic, suprahuman characters.

Editing

A *shot* is what is produced by a single operation of the camera—that is, what is seen from the time the camera is turned on until it is turned off.[9] Transition between shots and other manipulation of shots is affected by *editing,* (also called *cutting*), which can be done with a *straight cut* or with various types of *gradual cuts.*

Straight Cuts

In a straight cut a given image is replaced instantaneously by another. A straight cut may be used to replace one subject with another within a scene or to change scenes to a totally different time or place.

In Luchino Visconti's *Death in Venice* (1971) straight cuts link shots of the film's present in Venice with discussions of the nature of art held some time before in Germany. The cuts are quite sudden and one feels thrust into an unfamiliar situation. The suddenness of the cutting makes it difficult to adjust to the new place and time. These edited-in flashbacks are memories of painful arguments that leap into the mind of the film's protagonist in a fashion analogous to the way they leap onto the screen before us. In the case of this film, slow or other cuts in which the viewer is well-prepared for transitions to the past would not have been as powerful as the method used.

[9] See André Bazin, "The Evolution of the Language of Cinema." In *What Is Cinema?* vol. 1, trans. by Hugh Gray (Berkeley: University of California Press, 1967), pp. 25–40. Contains an illuminating discussion of the aesthetic potentials of action captured by a single shot.

Most straight cuts, however, are of the well-prepared variety, in which dialogue or visual elements at the end of one shot give some indication of what is coming in the next.

A cut can, of course, be made to a shot that closely approximates the preceding one.[10] When this type of transition is made, the flow of events seems to continue uninterruptedly. In general, *well-prepared straight cuts* contribute to a film's unity.

Another form of straight cut is the *jump cut,* in which part of the action is left out and one sees only part of an event. Most movies depict only parts of actions like walking, talking, fighting, or running, since it is unnecessary to see every step in order to have a sense of a whole event. A jump cut, however, omits so much of an action that the omission becomes the dominant event: for example, in shot 1 a character starts to turn slowly to the right; in shot 2 the character is completely turned and across the room. The typical reaction from movie audiences is that something has been left out. A comic chase may be absurdly funny precisely because too much of the action is left out. In a fantasy, a series of jump cuts can give an unnatural quality to events (see pages 65–72).

Gradual Cuts

Gradual cuts take a variety of forms. One is the *fade,* in which the image on the screen gradually disappears *(fade-out)* or appears *(fade-in)*. At one time it was common practice to deal with problematic situations (as in the case of a romantic scene in which the next logical event might provoke problems with the censor) by simply fading out and leaving everything to the viewer's imagination.

While seen only occasionally today, a style of gradual cutting that was popular during the early years of film is *irising*. In this technique, a circular space on a black screen expands *(iris-in)* to reveal a scene, or contracts *(iris-out)* until the scene is obliterated, and the screen then goes black.

The irising technique was used in the expressionistic film *The Cabinet of Dr. Caligari* (Robert Wiene, 1919). Throughout the film circular patterns are symbolic of chaos. Where irising began and ended a happy carnival sequence, an underlying feeling of chaos was created.[11] In this case irising was used to subtly increase the tension set up earlier in the film.

A *wipe* is a gradual-editing technique in which, generally, a new image moves slowly across the screen, its leading edge gradually excluding the old image. Though this type of transition is rather obvious and obtrusive, it can be used to heighten a sense of motion. One way this is accomplished is to cut on a subject in motion and to have the wipe move in the same direction, so as to continue the motion on the screen.

---

[10] Burch, *Theory of Film Practice,* p. 37.
[11] Siegfried Kracauer, *From Caligari to Hitler* (Princeton, N.J.: Princeton University Press, 1947), pp. 73–74

The *dissolve* is a gradual cut that is often used to increase a film's unity. In this cut the preceding image fades gradually from the screen while the new image gradually replaces it. Since both images are visible simultaneously, there is a strong tendency to compare or contrast the two.

The Last Picture Show (Peter Bogdanovich, 1971) made extensive use of the dissolve as a unifying factor. The final dissolve in the film is the most striking. Sonny (played by Timothy Bottoms) wants to leave his desolate, stifling home town, Anarene, after an accumulation of disheartening incidents that include the death of a father-figure, the annulment of his marriage, and the accidental death of a deaf-mute friend. But he cannot, and he resumes an affair with a middle-aged married woman. One feels that he will never leave and that his existence will be drab, desolate, and terribly limited. A shot of Sonny holding the married woman's hand in passive acceptance of his situation dissolves into a shot of the main street of Anarene, its café and movie house closed. The dissolve places the two images before us and forcefully marks the comparison between the life of the man and of the town.

Still another form of gradual cutting is the *overlap.* To bring about this mode of transition, part of an action already shown before a cut is repeated after the cut. This editing device tends to break up our sense of continuity and strikes us as artificial because it deviates from our experience of action in everyday life.

Eisenstein's *October* (1928) contains many examples of this editing style. In the famous drawbridge sequence, overlaps are used to express the theme that the rebels are innocent victims in the rebellion. As the sequence begins, government troops are firing on a group of rebellious people who are running across a drawbridge to escape the assault. As the drawbridge slowly opens, a white horse pulling a wagon is shot. The horse stumbles and falls near the center of the bridge. We then see the fall from a different angle, and then, again, the horse stumbling. Next, the film cuts to a bourgeois woman breaking one of the flags of the rebels, which is followed by a cut back to a side view of the falling horse with less of an overlap (that is, shorter) than the previous shot. The next cut is to a group of women attacking one of the rebels. The last cut is to a shot of the horse after the fall. Later in the sequence overlapping is again used when the horse is shown first hanging precariously as the sides of the bridge move toward their highest angle, then falling into the water below. The rebels' flags are next shown as they are thrown into the river. In the following shot we see the horse again hit the water. Finally we see a newspaper that had belonged to one of the rebels sink beneath the surface of the river.

Because the horse is shown so prominently in this sequence about the rebels, we associate the latter with his position as an innocent bystander in the rebellion. It is by comparison, with overlap being used for emphasis, that one of this film's major themes is communicated.

Transition Without Cuts

In addition to the foregoing types of editing, which involve cuts, there are modes of transition that involve no cutting. A *swish pan,* a very rapid panning from one object or space to another, creates a blur that can be tantamount to a cut.

Orson Welles made many of the transitions in his television movie *Fountain of Youth* (1958) by using the swish pan between scenes. In this very stagy and deliberately unreal story, the swish pan transitions worked well. The use of other forms of editing, which could have successfully "hidden" transitions between scenes, might have created a feeling of realism. That feeling would have been in conflict with the tongue-in-cheek quality in evidence throughout the production.

Basis for the Cut

An indefinite number of factors motivate editing. Some of the most readily apparent are as follows: to provide variety; to change scenes where the story calls for it; to eliminate unwanted parts of the action; to establish exciting or dramatic relationships that would not otherwise be possible, owing to the limitations of actors and stunt men (as when editing gives the illusion that the hero is rushing down a river toward rapids when in fact he is nowhere near the dangerous spot).

More subtle uses of editing have to do with making it another of the aesthetic devices of the film. These more artistic aspects of editing are discussed below.

Continuity Editing   Editing may help establish or preserve continuity; it can also disrupt continuity. A cut may be obvious, even blatant, or it may be relatively hidden from the viewer's awareness. The motives for preserving continuity include maintaining the flow of action and making clear the locations of things and the directions in which they are moving. Continuity is preserved either by contrasting or comparing what comes at the end of one shot with what comes at the beginning of the next.

A frequent style of cutting made on the basis of similarity and with the motive of preserving continuity is the *cut on motion.* This method has the actor or object making similar movements just before the cut and just after it. These movements must be such that they rather emphatically attract the viewer's attention. They should be motions in the same direction or of the same type or having other similarities. Cutting on these similar motions increases the likelihood that the viewer will be unconscious of the cut while his or her attention remains with the flow of the action.

The political film *Z* (1969) by Costa-Gavras makes extensive use of cutting on motion to maintain the flow of action in a scene where corrupt generals face an unyielding prosecutor who aims to get at the truth. Each general who comes before the prosecutor is asked the same questions. Rapid cutting timed on their similar motions gives a high degree of continuity to the sequence. The way their responses to the interrogation flow together becomes a visual metaphor for the preplanned character of their evasions.

Chris Marker's *La Jetée* (1963), unique in that it is composed almost entirely of stills, has a science-fiction motif, with characters who are survivors of an atomic war. The stills, embodying fragments of the lives of the characters, are used by them in an attempt to recapture the past. The stills supply the substance of the dead world they seek. Though confronted with a series of stills in all but one short sequence, the audience nevertheless is given a strong sense of motion by the cuts from one still to the next. The one scene where motion occurs comes at the end of a series of fluid cuts of a sleeping woman when her eyes flutter open. After relating to nothing but stills, viewers are typically surprised to find a character moving and realize how thoroughly they have accepted the illusion of motion.

Cutting via a theme is another way of achieving continuity. In Nichols' *The Graduate* continuity cutting was expressive of the main character's awareness of the world around him. It is Ben's first summer after having graduated from college. His feeling of alienation is made visible through the editing. One sequence involves intercutting scenes at his family's home with scenes of Ben's nightly meetings with Mrs. Robinson to make a smooth continuum. A shot of Ben jumping onto a rubber raft in his parents' pool gives way to a shot of him jumping onto a bed and into the welcoming arms of Mrs. Robinson. This in turn yields to a shot of him shaving while trying to explain to his mother where he spends his nights. The effect is twofold: The theme unifies the shots, and the editing is expressive of the theme.

Sound can also serve as the basis for linking shots. Music often functions as a bridge over transitions. In this type of editing a musical theme in one scene continues into the next, even though the scene may be of a different place or time. In *The Graduate* the music of Simon and Garfunkel continues on uninterruptedly as Ben, in shot after shot, races about California searching for the girl he loves. Here music lends unity to what otherwise might have been a series of repetitive shots of Ben in his car on the road.

Overlapping dialogue sometimes is used to smooth over a difficult transition while maintaining the flow of events. On several occasions in *Muriel* Resnais has the dialogue of a scene obtrude into the preceding one. At first it is difficult for the audience to grasp the connection between what is being said and what they see. By the time they are able to identify who is speaking, and where and when, the new scene, with its synchronized visuals and sound, has commenced.

Dissimilarity can also be a source of effective editing. In such cases, contrast provides the bridge across the cut. In *The Godfather* (Francis Ford Coppola, 1972) a series of cuts back and forth between a baptism and a bloody ambush are connected by contrast. The moral declarations of the Godfather at the baptism ritual, alternating with the criminal activities taking place elsewhere under his orders, underscore the hypocrisy required by his new position of power.

Discontinuity Editing   Discontinuity as a manner of connecting shots also has its aesthetic uses. Editing discontinuity creates a marked alteration in one or more aspects of a film's action. The scene may shift abruptly to some different place or time. Actions may seem to be broken up or downright incoherent.

An editing technique known as *mismatching* supplies a ready mechanism for achieving discontinuity. Mismatching (of shots in sequence) can be done with respect to virtually any feature of a film's action: the direction in which action is moving; the location of persons and things in the setting; the speed with which persons or things move; or the size, shape, color, volume, texture, and sound of things. Where the context of a film dictates that a feature be disconcerting or even incoherent, discontinuity editing may be just the right artistic solution.

Imagine a sequence in which the following occurs: (1) An actor facing screen-right speaks to another (unseen) actor. (2) The second actor, alone and also facing screen-right, replies to the greeting and starts talking to the first actor. (3) The first actor responds to the remarks, again facing screen-right. Such a mismatched shot series is disconcerting to the viewer. This is so because editing has usually been employed to give action on the screen a character similar to that of everyday life.

Imagine yet another shot series: (1) a group of three men, including the film's star, who is on the left; (2) a close-up of the star, now on the right. If nothing in the visual elements or dialogue indicates a reason for this shift in the star's location, such editing would produce a discontinuity that would be quite disruptive.

In Jean-Luc Godard's *Breathless* (1959) a chase sequence includes a series of mismatchings of screen direction. The hero of the film (played by Jean-Paul Belmondo) is in a car chase with the police. At one point in the chase the direction in which he is going is screen-right, but the police chase Belmondo by going screen-left. His movement, therefore, does not match that of his pursuers. A convention governing the portrayal of direction in many films (which this sequence in *Breathless* violates) is that pursued and pursuer move in the same direction. To accomplish this matching of screen direction, a 180-degree rule is observed: The camera, in capturing the movements of pursued and pursuer, stays on the same side of the street as both pass; it does not cross an imaginary 180-degree line that runs down the middle of the street. In *Breathless* Belmondo's car is shown from one side of the street doing right as it passes by the camera. Then the camera crosses the street (thereby crossing the 180-degree line) and photographs the police passing (to the left) on their motorcycles in pursuit of Belmondo.

Breathless contains other mismatchings. In one shot series, in which Belmondo walks toward a closet, the mismatching is achieved by omission of parts of the action. This editing effect is the jump cut mentioned above. The aesthetic uses of discontinuity in screen direction and in the portrayal of an action will be explored in detail in the discussion (pages 62–74) of Godard's camera style.

Graphic Editing   Some directors, like the Russian master filmmaker and theoretician Sergei Eisenstein, have worked out elaborate systems of cutting that are grounded on graphic structures—two-dimensional compositions much like those in painting and, like them, dealing with qualities such as balance, proportion, and symmetry. Graphic editing joins shots on the basis of the two-dimensional patterns they contain.

In the "Odessa Steps" sequence in *The Battleship Potemkin,* Eisenstein portrays the troops driving the people down the steps in a manner timed to match the graphic qualities of the steps. The soldiers' mechanically paced movements as they march in formation have a rhythm and orderliness like the intervals of the steps, which contrast with the confusion and disorder of the fleeing people. Cutting between these graphically disparate movements visually emphasizes the conflict represented.

At one point in the assault a child is hit. His mother carries him toward the advancing soldiers, pleading with them to stop. As she approaches, their shadows fall across her, and she dies under their shadows. As the soldiers continue, their shadows become relentless diagonal lines that cut across screen space, symbolically connecting the shooting of the woman holding her child with the actions of the troops against the people.

Later in the advance, the woman with a baby carriage is shot. A circular movement of the head, which marks her reaction to the pain, forms the unifying basis for editing the shot series, which ends with her fall and the famous passage of the baby carriage bumping down the Odessa Steps. Before the circular movement of her head is completed a cut is made to a close-up of the wheels of the baby carriage, their circular shapes dominating the screen. A cut back to the mother shows her head as it completes the circular motion. Then a cut is made to an extreme close-up of her hands clutching her waist where she has been shot. Her hands surround a circular belt buckle as she writhes in pain. Her motions throughout this shot series are rhythmically similar—a further connection between them.

The term *sequence* has had a central place in the language used to describe editing. Though the term *editing* admits of some vagueness, it can be counted on to refer to the portrayal of a complete action, that is, a sequence of events with a beginning, middle, and end.[12] Although a sequence usually involves editing, it need not. Orson Welles' *Touch of Evil,* for example, contains a sequence in a simple long shot that opens the film (see pages 43–46).

Where editing does play a role, a sequence is identifiable as a series of shots that are connected to form a whole that establishes some action, situation, or dilemma, develops it, and then brings it to a close. The shots that make up the Odessa Steps scenes in Eisenstein's *The Battleship Potemkin* constitute a sequence. It establishes a conflict between the advancing troops and people, develops the situation into a full-scale assault, and brings it to a close with the driving of the people from the steps and the response of the battleship. Though

[12] The best discussion of *complete action* is to be found in Aristotle, *Poetics.*

the action continues with the battleship preparing for an assault on the Czar's fleet, the audience feels that the initial situation has been brought to a close.

Plastic Editing   Plastic editing connects shots on the basis of the three-dimensional qualities of the things shown in them. Editing grounded in three-dimensional qualities connects shots by matching (or opposing) volumes, depth relationships, movements, and the like.

In *October,* Eisenstein shows a crowd pulling down a large and politically important statue as part of their demonstration of support of the ruling provisional government and of hatred for the old rulers. As people mount the statue, throw ropes over it, and pull off its head, arms, and legs, the viewer has a vivid sense of its volume. Gigantic in substance and form, as contrasted to the tiny forms of the people, it is expressive of the enormous force that the people are attempting to overthrow.

In a later *October* sequence, the people have become disenchanted with the provisional government. Lenin has kept his fateful date at the Finland Station and is now ready to lead a revolution. As the people mass about their leader, he is shown above them from a low shooting angle that gives him increased stature. A reverse angle is then employed, with the camera above and behind Lenin and shooting down on the crowd. This angle also lends qualities of stature and dominance to Lenin. Cutting from below Lenin to above him conveys the idea that, regardless of the spatial relations of Lenin to the people, in the depth of the film's space he is superior to them.

After Lenin meets the people they stage a demonstration against the provisional government. Their collective movements through screen space make visible the order and will of their resistance. Edited so as to emphasize a gradual process of gathering together, the scenes show the various groups of people slowly but surely moving toward the formation of a single line of marchers. The line they form becomes a vector that cuts through the depth of the screen and heads toward a confrontation with the authorities. When the conflict occurs, intercutting visually expresses the action. One shot depicts the dispersion of the people in every direction to escape the gunfire of government troops. A superimposed shot shows a gunner firing every which way. Both shots in this intercut series depict the action in three-dimensional terms.

Rhythmic Editing   Editing establishes a rhythmic pattern. Rapid and frequent cutting, which has a kind of staccato tempo, lends excitement to Godard's *Breathless.* By contrast, an absence of much editing (resulting in the camera dwelling on a situation for longer periods) contributes to the languid tone of Satyajit Ray's *Pather Panchali* (1955); a tone that is fitting for this portrayal of the slow-moving life of a family in India.

Cutting rhythms correspond to musical rhythms in many films. In the title sequence of John Schlesinger's *Midnight Cowboy* (1969) the viewer is given a highly compact survey of the central character's circumstances and the reasons he has decided to leave Texas for New York City. To the lyrics and music of the song "Everybody's Talkin' at Me," a series of rapid cuts show the "cowboy" working at and quitting a menial job as a dishwasher in a sleazy café, buying his colorful cowboy outfit, and preparing for the move to the big city. The correspondence in rhythm between editing and song prompts us to apply the words of the song to the character's situation and gives a flow to events that ensures our involvement in the action when he arrives in New York.

A nonmusical notion of rhythm is employed in talking about the order in which shots from different camera positions are edited together. For a rather long period (1940s–1950s), Hollywood had a standard way of cutting together long, medium, and close-up views of subjects. The opening shot of a sequence gave a perspective long enough to make it relatively easy to get one's bearings within a scene. This was known as the *establishing shot.* Following this long shot, a transition was made to a middle-distance view, and then finally the editing left us with a close-up of the action. In such a shot series the three camera positions were shown for a roughly equal length of time.

Reversal of this standard cutting rhythm in subsequent years provided a refreshing change in style. Now the viewers may be thrust into the center of an action with a close-up shot—as in the opening series of shots in Coppola's *The Conversation* (1974)—only later to get their bearings via a long-shot perspective.

The relative length of time spent on each shot in a series can be indicative of the importance of each shot. The style of John Cassavetes in films like *Faces* (1968), *Husbands* (1969), and *Minnie and Moscowitz* (1971) is to emphasize the importance of what is shown in close-ups by giving such camera positions more time than medium or long shots. In *Minnie and Moscowitz,* in a scene where Minnie talks with an older woman about their love lives, much more time is spent on close-ups of Minnie's face than on medium or long views of her. This editing (many close shots) indicates to the viewer that what is revealed in this conversation is of real importance.

In Antonioni's *L'Avventura* (1960) a long shot of people searching for a lost woman on an island is held for a much longer time than shots from other camera positions in the shot series. The long shot presents a compact image of the collective frustration and isolation of the searchers. All are shown from the back, all facing in somewhat different directions, as they gaze across the terrain of the island in search of some sign of the missing woman. Again, the length of this shot relative to the brevity of the others engages the audience's attention.

Where pacing of close-up, medium, and long shots is roughly equal in length, it is natural to regard the content of such shots as being of the same importance, all other things being equal.

The 400 Blows, *1959. Courtesy Janus Films*

Optical Effects

Another category of visual elements is that of optical effects. Some of the effects grouped under this heading can be accomplished in the process of shooting. Some—such as the fades and dissolves discussed above—are produced either in the film-processing laboratory *or* in the camera during shooting. And some—such as the wipes discussed above, and certain multiple exposures and freeze frames—can be produced *only* in the laboratory. Important optical effects, other than those discussed earlier, are: change in image size, change in object position, optical zoom, skip framing, double framing, freeze framing, superimpositions, and matting.

Part of an image can be altered optically so as to enlarge or reduce it or to remove unwanted elements from it. Such a *change in image size* would be advantageous where the relative size of objects is indicative of the dominance of one thing over another. Demands of composition (such as balance) may call for the removal of part of an image.

A shot can be printed so that it is reversed inside the frame. Rudolf Arnheim points out that compositions work most effectively when the objects of greatest interest in them are placed along the diagonal running from bottom left to top right.[13] An *optical reversal* that would result in distribution of the elements in a shot in this fashion might, therefore, be useful aesthetically.

---

[13] Arnheim, *Art and Visual Perception,* p. 22.

An *optical zoom* has uses parallel to those of the zoom lens (pages 8–9), though image clarity of the former is somewhat less than that of the latter. To produce an optical zoom, the frames making up an image are progressively enlarged in the laboratory, to give an effect approximating that of shooting a scene with a zoom lens. For a naturalistic film in which a zoom-in is needed, an optically produced zoom may be better because it avoids the distortions of space resulting from use of a zoom lens.

Fast motion and slow motion are produced optically by processes called, respectively, *skip framing* and *double framing*. Skip framing speeds up action by omitting some of the frames of a sequence making up a shot. In double framing each frame is printed twice. This prolongs the action photographed, giving an effect of slow motion, though one in which movement is jerky and abrupt.

In *freeze framing,* the same frame is repeated over and over, stopping the action entirely. At the end of François Truffaut's *The 400 Blows* (1959) the flight from the juvenile authorities of a delinquent boy is suddenly arrested in a memorable freeze frame. This shot, against a background of ocean, leaves the audience with the impression that time has been temporarily stopped for the boy, but that it will flow on again in many directions.

Images may be piled one on the other by use of the optical technique of *superimposition.* The effect is something like that of some metaphors, in which several poetic ideas are compacted into a single image. In film, when two or more images are to be connected in one shot, superimposition may be the proper vehicle. A character reflecting on her past, for example, could be shown with the faces of several people close to her superimposed over a shot of her own face, giving the impression that she is seeing her friends in her mind's eye. Superimpositions call attention to themselves and so must be sparingly employed to avoid blunting their effect when they *are* used.

Persona, *1966*

Superimposed titles have become a creative aspect of the motion picture. In the past, audiences had to endure a long stretch of film credits before the movie proper appeared; today it is far more common to have a movie begin with some arresting action and to superimpose the titles as the action progresses. Sometimes titles are integrated into the action, bearing some graphic connection with it. *Barbarella* (Roger Vadim, 1968), a science-fiction film with sexual overtones, has a voyeuristic opening in which the titles are peepholes through which the audience tries to see Barbarella (Jane Fonda) as she disrobes and puts on a space suit.

Matting is a type of superimposition in which a foreground action shot of one place is superimposed upon a background shot of another place and/or time. Remarkable examples of how convincing this process can be are certain chase sequences set against backgrounds of the ultramodern city Brasília in De Broca's *That Man from Rio* (1964). Though the chases (foreground) were staged on sets in France, the action appears as if it took place in the streets (background) of this dazzling city.

Mise en Scène

The term *"mise en scène,"* which originated in the theatre, refers to the combined impression given by (1) the actors, their performances, make-up, and costumes, and (2) the setting, including props and lighting. With allowances for differences between the media, this term applies both to theatre and film.

Actor-Centered Features

Actors communicate their characters' feelings, intentions, desires, and ideas in a variety of ways. Dialogue is often among the most important. The meaning of what the characters say in films is, of course, something that we understand by relying directly upon our knowledge of the language. One cannot underestimate the role dialogue-meaning has in revealing the situation, advancing the plot, developing a theme, or making character portrayal more effective. There is, however, another aesthetically important aspect of dialogue—namely, dialogue as sound quality apart from meaning. Actors can communicate much about their characters and a film's situation by such qualities of voice as intensity, texture, pitch, and rhythm (see Chapter 2).

Body language is another mode of actor communication. Posture, gait, gestures, mannerisms, and the distance an actor puts between himself or herself and other characters or objects are all expressive of feelings, attitudes, and relationships. The comedy of a silent actor such as Buster Keaton is a collage of shrugs, slouches, stares, stone faces, pratfalls, and acrobatic maneuvers. With these actions of his body he expresses the spectrum of human emotions.

Dialogue and body language are, of course, features of acting that film shares with theatre. There are, in addition, features of film acting that differentiate it from acting in the theatre. These features center around the relation of the actor to the camera.

One of these cinematic features of acting is that of being photogenic. The term "photogenic" does not mean simply "glamorous," but rather capable of showing to best advantage on camera. This means that the qualities a director wants in an actor's face must not only be present on her face as she performs but must also be of a kind that can be captured by the camera. One of these qualities might be the beauty of a Marilyn Monroe. Or it might be the hardness and coldness of a Bogart, the craggy-textured face of a Michel Simon, even the striking ugliness of a Charles Laughton as he plays Quasimodo in *The Hunchback of Notre Dame* (1939).

The actor must also be sensitive to the presence of the camera. For example, small facial movements, which would go unnoticed in ordinary life (or in the theatre), can be captured in close-up with quite distracting results. When an actor successfully coordinates his movements, close-ups can be used to provide more subtle forms of expression than are possible in theatrical performances. Where actors in a theatre must "project" to reach everyone present, actors in film may rely on very small gestures to communicate a character's life to an audience.

The actor's make-up and costume must be attuned to the character projected. They may be central to the role created, even the single most important *mise en scène* quality of a film. For instance, Chaplin's make-up, including his tiny mustache, his cane, hat, rumpled suit, and run-down shoes, became a trademark that identified his famous comic character Charlie. His unique style of body language was enhanced by these elements of make-up and costume. When the little tramp trotted about made-up and dressed in this way, his every movement had potential for hilarity.

Modern Times, *1936*

Make-up and costume, like all other actor-centered features, have to be adjusted to the shifting camera viewpoints brought about by altered camera position, altered shooting angle, camera movement, and editing. Like the actor's face, they must continue to show up as wanted even as the camera shifts. A changed camera position can also make an actor's appearance spoil the compositional values of a scene.

Setting and Lighting

Filmmakers can use an interior or exterior setting as it is, alter it, or build their own sets. Shooting on location (rather than on a studio's sets) lends authenticity to a scene. Such "natural" settings may have to be altered, however, to obtain necessary light or to make them appear more real or attractive. For example, reflectors can be placed so as to alter the available light of a natural setting.

Painting or otherwise altering the colors of objects in natural settings is also done to increase certain effects. Some of the most memorable scenes in Antonioni's *Blow-Up* (1967) were filmed in a park where a murder occurred. The park's grass had a lushness that was enhanced by paint to emphasize the contrast between the beauty of the setting and the shocking murder that took place there.

Settings may also be altered by *back-projection,* in which shots of a setting—exterior or interior—are projected onto a semitransparent screen on the other side of which the action is staged. Back-projection, seldom effective, is used infrequently today.

Setting may depart almost totally from the everyday appearance of things. *The Cabinet of Dr. Caligari* stages its action against settings that are highly expressionistic. The lines of buildings appear bent, windows are oddly shaped, and doorways look like decorations on the walls rather than openings in them. Perspective is altered so as to make the film's environments appear less three-dimensional.

The setting in *Dr. Caligari* gives expression to the inner feelings of characters. Where an impressionistic film attempts to capture the surface features of the real, an expressionistic film like *Dr. Caligari* presents us with visual qualities that embody *feeling* about reality.

Lighting has much to do with the shape and character of a setting. Light not only allows us to see that there are objects in the film space but also how they are shaped, in what directions they are turned, and the distances that separate them. Crucial in conveying these qualities and relations of objects is the interplay of light and shadow.[14] A factor related to that interplay is *fall-off,* the rapidity with which the two—light and shadow—shade off into each other. When fall-off is marked or rapid, we recognize the object as having a sharp edge or corner; when gradual or slow, as having a curved surface. Though

---

[14] Ibid., pp. 292–322; for a host of useful concepts of lighting.

The Cabinet of Dr. Caligari, *1919*

quite subtle and ordinarily not noticed, fall-off is constantly at work in our perception of objects in a film.

The most important lighting sources in terms of the aesthetic uses of light are *key light* and *fill light.* The key light is the main and most intense source of light on a subject when it is photographed. In the classic use of the key light it is placed high, to one side of the camera, and in front of the subject. From this position it provides a hard, direct light on the subject, producing deep, well-defined shadows. The key light can, however, be placed in a variety of positions. Where a character moves about a setting, there may be several key lights, one for each of the locations.

The fill light, generally placed near the camera on the side opposite the key light, serves to lighten the shadows created by the key light. The fill light, then, is used for altering fall-off.

How a subject looks in a film depends in part upon the distribution of brightness in the setting. In the glistening-white daylight world of the city of Algiers in *The Battle of Algiers,* an all-white object will not stand out; the contrary is true in the mod world of reds, greens, and blues of *Blow-Up.* It is the same with light apart from color. A subject illuminated by a bright light will stand out in direct proportion to the dimness of the fill light; the closer the intensity of the fill light to that of the key light, the less conspicuous the subject. Thus, an evaluation of light requires, in the first place, analysis of the relation between key and fill light.

"Key," with reference to light, is also used with its commoner connotation. There are *low- and high-key lightings,* which have to do with qualities of the overall lighting situation. When overall lighting is low-key, most of the setting is in shadow, leaving only a few areas well-illuminated. High-key lighting, on the other hand, has relatively little shadow, illumination is soft and diffuse, and the overall tone of the setting is bright. Between low- and high-key lighting falls *graduated tonality lighting,* which has many gradations of grays (in black-and-white films), weak shadows, and soft light, evenly distributed.

In addition to these uses of the term "key" in relation to lighting, there is also a usage relating to the emotional tone of a scene. In this sense, high-key scenes are intense and highly emotional, and low-key scenes less so. Lighting often plays a role in the emotional tone of a scene. However, there is no direct correspondence between high- and low-key lighting and emotionally high- and low-key scenes. High-key lighting contributes to low-key emotional tone in Lucas' portrayal of the future in *THX 1138* (1971). Low-key lighting contributes to high-key emotional tone in the Oklahoma dust bowl scenes in Ford's *The Grapes of Wrath* (1940).

A third principal light is the *back light.* When a scene is back lit, light comes from behind and, usually, from above the subject. If a back light is the only key light in the scene, the outlines of a figure will be visible but details of the face will be relatively indistinguishable. Combining the back light used as a key light with another key light placed to the side of the subject (a *kicker light*—one placed to the side and lower than the back light) adds three-dimensionality to the subject by separating it visually from the background. By contrast, lighting directly from the front tends to flatten the appearance of things, softening the modeling of faces and, on the whole, diminishing the viewer's sense of texture and relief. Placing key light to the side tends to outline a subject, as in Norman McLaren's depiction of a dance in *Pas de Deux* (1968), memorable for its side-lighted forms that move in an abstract space.

Low-key lighting has often been used in conjunction with other visual elements to give a sinister look to locales. When Orson Welles made his cinematic version of Franz Kafka's novel *The Trial* (1964), he photographed many scenes in low-key lighting. This helped to give the sets qualities of darkness, confinement, and sinister foreboding; qualities altogether appropriate for this bleak nightmare story of a man who is accused of and tried for a crime whose nature is not disclosed to him.

Low-key lighting was an essential feature of a whole style in the American film—the *film noir.* This "dark film" era of the 40s, during and after World War II, produced such films as the private-eye thrillers of Bogart (*The Maltese Falcon,* 1941), the lone-wolf story (*The Lost Weekend,* 1945), the realistic urban drama (*The House on 92nd Street,* 1945), and the psychological-exploration melodrama (*White Heat,* 1949). It was in the shadows created by low-key lighting in these *films noir* that the protagonists had their rendezvous, ambushes, and love affairs. The sinister, moody, often tense atmospheres of the *film noir* would be unthinkable without low-key lighting.

The Maltese Falcon, *1941*

High-key lighting in musicals like Jacques Demy's *The Young Girls of Rochefort* (1967) or Stanley Donen's *Singin' in the Rain* (1952) creates a warm, sunny, lively, optimistic atmosphere that suits the tone of a world where characters often dance instead of walk and sing rather than talk, where opportunity lies just around the corner, and where everything works out well in the end.

Bright lighting can be carried to extremes. The above-mentioned nightmare distortion of the opening scene in *Wild Strawberries* (obtained by use of high-contrast stock) is also partly attributable to overlighting, which heightens the harsh contrasts and coarseness of the unreal image.

The musical *Cabaret* (1972), directed by Bob Fosse, and the drama *The Blue Angel* (1930), directed by Joseph von Sternberg, provide useful illustrations of how the foregoing characteristics of *mise en scène* work together in unifying a film's action. These films make excellent use of acting, make-up, costume, setting, and lighting for their portrayal of German life in the throes of its 1920s decadence.

Sets used for *Cabaret's* scenes in the Kit Kat Club contain garish colors and opulent decor, while lighting is extremely bright. The actors' performances are marked by the tasteless use of make-up and costumes: The master of ceremonies (Joel Grey) wears heavy, white make-up and a tuxedo, while Sally Bowles (Liza Minelli) wears heavy lipstick, huge eyelashes, green nail polish, and scanty, beaded dresses.

In a long series of cross cuts, the world of the Kit Kat Club is compared to the world outside. Scenes of Grey and Minelli performing on the club's gaudy, overlit stage alternate with such scenes as proto-Nazi thugs beating a man in a dark alley. The *mise en scène* qualities chosen for scenes in the Kit Kat Club express visually the false gaiety, decadence, and fear prevalent in pre-Nazi Germany.

In *The Blue Angel* a middle-aged high-school teacher (Emil Jannings), trying to prevent his pupils from visiting Lola, the star entertainer (Marlene Dietrich) of the Blue Angel Club, becomes himself so enthralled with her that he forsakes his former life and endures degradation to follow her.

Sets in the Blue Angel Club—narrow, cramped interiors—give a feeling of confinement. The stage where Lola performs is choked with props, and the overabundant decor (similar to that of *Cabaret*) is expressive of the decadent display that marked the period.

Dietrich's performance, costume, make-up, and manner of relating to other characters (especially the teacher) combine to project detachment and cynicism. Her every movement conveys moral looseness. Her clothes are openly provocative and her make-up is exaggerated, and she sings the cynical tunes of the era in her throaty, mysterious voice. The *mise en scène* characteristics of the interiors of the Blue Angel Club expose the viewer to the decadent world the film depicts.

sound

Sound—texture, location, type, relation, and its absence—constitutes another means of appreciating and understanding the action of a film. Sound in film includes *dialogue* and *music*.

Orson Welles' *Citizen Kane* (1940), which makes brilliant use of sound, will be used to illustrate many of the points discussed in this chapter.

Dialogue

Dialogue is probably the sound feature to which movie audiences respond most readily. Nothing in a film is more accessible to us than the meaning of the words spoken by the characters. That we grasp the meaning to be found in dialogue is a necessity in an overwhelming number of films. Words also exhibit most of the other sound qualities found in film. These qualities will be discussed later in this chapter.

Music

Music can establish mood, atmosphere, and tone. It can also serve as a device for transitions between shots, as when it continues while the scene shifts to a new time or place. The style of music functions in many films to communicate the era portrayed. Music's place in film is not, however, restricted to a role outside of the action; it can be brought into the action by an actress when she switches on a radio, sings, or plays an instrument.

Citizen Kane contains a remarkable variety of musical styles, beginning with the march that accompanies the titles of the newsreel *News on the March.* Because marches usually accompanied actual newsreels, this use in *Citizen Kane* gives the newsreel more authenticity.

A brooding, melancholy theme used in the opening sequence lends mystery and foreboding to the portrayal of Kane's death in his opulent pleasure palace Xanadu. These qualities are created again when similar music accompanies the scene in which Thompson, a reporter searching for the real story of Kane's life, talks to Kane's second wife, Susan Alexander. At this point, the identity of Citizen Kane is wrapped in mystery, and the music cues our recognition of this.

The film includes grand opera. (Kane buys an opera house to promote the talentless Susan as an opera star, in order to have the prestige of being associated with the operatic world.) Show tunes are played and danced by Kane and his newspaper staff to celebrate its success and to establish Kane's worldliness and extroversion. Jazz is sung at a picnic by entertainers who project a warm, natural feeling in counterpoint with a violent argument between Kane and Susan.

Aspects of Film Sound

Texture

The crucial textural features of sound are *intensity* (loud, soft), *pitch* (high, low), and *character* (hollow, harsh, soft).

Scenes in *Citizen Kane* typically open with loud, assaultive sounds that engage the audience and fix their attention on the new screen images. For example, from the quiet closing of the sequence in which Kane dies, a cut is made to the newsreel and its blaring march music.

Voices contrast in texture, as in the scene in which a voice teacher, using soft, well-modulated tones, instructs an inept, screeching Susan.

All the features of sound texture are at work in a scene at Kane's boyhood home in Colorado. His mother has decided to allow him to be adopted, so that he may have opportunities she can't provide. Sound texture is an index of the state of family relations at the time. The voice of Kane's mother is loudest, harshest, and highest pitched, indicating her dominance over Kane's father.

The father's voice is the quietest, gentlest, and most modulated in the family. The child Kane's voice is intermediate with respect to these features, implying personality traits acquired from both his parents.

Location

Sounds in a film are perceived as close-up, at a medium distance, and at a long distance from the camera. They also may seem to be either on or off screen. When on screen, sounds work in conjunction with visual elements to delimit the space in which the film's action occurs. When off screen, sounds have expressive potentials quite like those of offscreen visual images (pages 14–19).

Sound in the engulfing halls of Xanadu is faint, and thereby located as distant. One feels the vast distances that physically as well as psychologically separate Kane and Susan in this place. By contrast, sounds in the newspaper office are loud and interpenetrating, giving a sense of the confining space in which the newspaper staff works.

In the above-mentioned picnic scene, the pace of cutting between the singers and the argument between Kane and Susan gradually quickens until Kane silences Susan's complaining by slapping her. At that moment, a woman's cry is heard, seemingly off screen. It may be a cry of fear or of ecstasy. Its source is unknown and we can only imagine its location and meaning, and in its ambiguity it engages our imagination.

Type

On some occasions, when background music (music not arising directly from the action) accompanies a scene, it lends an unreal or unnatural quality to the action. Offscreen narration often plays a similar role. To the contrary, sounds that are identified as part of the natural setting (such as dialogue, laughter, footsteps, car rumblings, bird calls) ordinarily contribute a realistic or natural tone to what is portrayed.

In *Citizen Kane,* the reality of natural sounds is used for a scene in the Thatcher Memorial Library to reveal the character of Kane's overbearing guardian. While the reporter searches through Thatcher's records for a clue to the meaning of Kane's last word—"Rosebud"—we hear hollowly echoing sounds in the library (dialogue, footsteps, turning of the pages in Thatcher's diary) that are expressive of the emptiness of Thatcher the man.

Voice-over narration (the narrator not visible) by the people whom the reporter interviews begins in the present and continues as the past is shown. This way of flashing back to what the person recollects of Kane puts the viewer at some distance from those past events. The voice-overs interrupt the realistic tone that is established at many places in the film.

Absence

The absence of sound can establish a mood, arrest an action, focus attention on crucial visual elements, and foster suspense. An absence of sound is used in the opening sequence of *Kane* to communicate the dominance of his presence. Just before he dies, Kane utters the mysterious word "Rosebud"; a silence follows that highlights the emptiness of the film's world without his commanding figure.

Silence also falls over Xanadu at the end of the film. The reporter, Thompson, having admitted his failure to discover the meaning of the word "Rosebud," has left. The camera dollies over the vast possessions that fill Xanadu's rooms. Except for the background music, there is no sound. We are left to contemplate this world of inanimate objects. The film has been full of scenes opening with loud, attention-attracting sounds of action, arguments, parties, and music. Silence now comes as a marked contrast. It is in this silence that the secret of "Rosebud" is revealed.

Relative to Other Elements

A sound may correspond to, contrast with, or be isolated from other features of a film (including other sounds). A sound and another sound or a visual element edited together can have a realistic or unexpected association (*synchronous* or *asynchronous,* respectively).

When sounds are edited together, some rhythmic pattern is almost inevitably established, even where the original component sounds are shapeless or chaotic. With care in the organization of sounds, distinctive rhythms can be created that have many of the qualities we associate with musical rhythms. Sound has also been used as a basis for transitions between shots.

A memorable piece of editing involving a correspondence of a sound with a visual element occurs in a scene in which the butler recalls the day Kane's second wife left him. His recollections are bracketed by the screech of a cockatoo at the beginning, representing Kane's agony concerning Susan's flight from Xanadu, and, at the end, a shot of Kane in despair reflected seemingly endlessly in a series of mirrors. The visual thereby matches the sound.

The picnic scene mentioned above is an example of sound (the jazz song) contrasted with another feature.

In the opening scene the camera moves into an extreme close-up, registering Kane's lips as he murmurs the mysterious word "Rosebud." The isolation of the word from all other sounds confers significance upon it appropriate to the central place it has in the film.

Though sound throughout *Kane* is mostly synchronous, there are occasions when it is asynchronous. An example of the latter is the light, jingling music heard as background while the Thatcher diary is perused by the reporter in the tomblike atmosphere of Thatcher's library.

Dialogue and other sounds of the environment can be coordinated to produce a rhythmic pattern. Action in *Citizen Kane* is marked throughout by a staccato rhythm. Scenes open in a hard, fast, loud fashion. Action is fast-paced, events occur abruptly, and characters come and go from the screen rapidly. This rhythm gives expression to the quality of Kane's world. A scene exhibiting these characteristics is that in which Kane assumes operation of the *Inquirer;* it is also filled with fascinating sound rhythms. Kane introduces himself and his two associates, Leland and Bernstein, to a bumbling, excitable man, Mr. Carter, who has been the managing editor of the paper. Kane and his associates bombard Carter with names, orders, and comments. Totally flustered, Carter turns this way and that, shaking hands with the wrong person, misidentifying others. Through all the confusion, sound is woven into rhythmic patterns. Kane's voice is like a rising and falling wave as he bellows out names and gives orders; Carter's stumbling efforts are marked by alternations between sweeping verbal cadences when he thinks he has it right and halting staccatos when he thinks he may be wrong.

Dialogue in *Citizen Kane* is often fragmented, with characters frequently interrupting one another. This dialogue rhythm is indicative of the fast-paced and competitive world in which the characters dwell. Fragmented speech also lends a realistic cast to the Senate Committee investigation of Thatcher: It seems natural for men whose time is so valuable to speak only in fragments.

In the scene where Boss Jim Geddes confronts Kane, Susan, and Kane's first wife Emily with his threat to expose an affair between Kane and Susan, fragmented speech indicates a painful lack of communication. Explanations are attempted but interruptions prevent their completion. The audience, knowing the relationship between Kane and Susan is innocent, feels frustration at the inability of Kane and Susan to communicate the truth to Emily.

Transitions in *Kane,* accomplished in a way that commands our attention, often use loud, harsh sounds as their basis. Many of the cuts are also made with sound in a way that deftly preserves continuity. Some fifteen years of Kane's adolescence are bridged with sound editing when, at the end of one shot, Thatcher wishes the boy Kane "Merry Christmas" and, at the beginning of the next, offers "and a Happy New Year" to Kane as a young man. In another such example Kane's applause for Susan's singing at their first meeting becomes the applause of his supporters at a political rally. Besides making the transition between these two different times and locations, this latter piece of sound editing serves to connect Kane's private life with his public life.

Interaction with Visual Elements

For a clear picture of how sound works in interaction with visual elements, it will be necessary to make a close examination of a small section of a film—in this case, the *tour de force* opening sequence from Orson Welles' *Touch of Evil,* which contains only one shot, a remarkable long take of some three minutes' duration. (Descriptions of the sequence are italicized, with certain emphasized terms in normal (roman) type. The analysis of the sequence is set in normal type.)

The camera focuses on a hand that is manipulating a time-bomb mechanism in screen center. We do not see the bomber's face. *Until the bomb is set, there is an* absence of sound. *Then we hear the faint ticking of the timing mechanism, and, while the camera fixes on the bomb, the sound of a woman's laughter in the distance.*

Sound is used in part to create the space of the film. The sound of the timing mechanism establishes a foreground, while the soft laughter in the distance establishes a background. Both sounds are soft and quiet. This similarity in *texture* and *volume* makes a comparison of the sounds' relative positions in the space rather easy. Had the laughter been loud it would have been more difficult to place it in relation to the bomb and its ticking.

Rhythmical drum music *begins just after the sound of laughter.* It establishes a tone of excitement. This rhythmical beat will continue until after the bomb has been planted, the bomber has disappeared, and the owner of the car in which the bomb has been placed gets into it.

The camera pans *sharply to a man and a woman walking through a distant archway toward the bomber, who dashes across the screen from right to left, leaving it open.* The audience's attention is then drawn deeper into the space by the presence of the man and woman. *The man and woman move from left to right. The bomber now moves back (also left to right, but in the foreground) very quickly. He looms larger and larger as he moves.* His looming appearance heightens our sense of the ominousness of the scene.

The action in these sections of the shot is not easily understood. What, for example, is the relation between the setting of the bomb and the man and woman in the distance? Against whom is the bomb to be used?

The bomber runs along a fence toward a car. The camera tracks *behind him at ground level. He places the bomb in the trunk of the car. The man and woman appear, get into the car, and drive off.* Now we know why the bomber has been startled, why he has been in such a rush, and against whom the bomb is directed (though we don't know who they are).

The camera lifts up, *the film's titles start, and music begins—an ominous theme. The camera* backs up *high behind a building adjoining the location. The camera* tracks left *along the top of the building as the film's titles continue in superimposition on its roof. The car then pulls away out of sight behind the building. When the track left along the top of the building is complete, the camera picks up the car just emerging from behind the building.* This appearance, disappearance, and reappearance of the car (with the camera and car moving at the same pace) develops a rhythm that contributes to the feeling (already established) that the camera has a suprahuman viewpoint—that is, that its view of the happenings it records is beyond that of human powers of observation. It cranes its neck up to get a sense of the whole location. It moves along the rooftops, staying out of sight, as it were, and hovering like a hummingbird. It varies from close-up (the setting of the bomb's timing device) to long shot (the couple on their way to their car). With the reinforcement provided by the ominous theme music, the camera's presence and movements lend an eerie quality to what is happening.

The shot continues, with the camera moving gradually down *(almost imperceptibly) to street level. At the same time, the car turns slowly into a main street.* This street is sharply defined by the effect of the natural setting. The arches along its sides converge in the distance, providing a kind of natural frame for the car as it pulls into screen center. The *lighting* helps to mark out the natural framing effect. *The camera* pulls ahead *of the car by about a block as the car's progress is temporarily impeded by a crossing cart.* Throughout this part of the shot, *camera movement* is motivated by *object movement* (first the bomber, now the car). *Next the camera moves even farther ahead of the car as it travels along the well-defined street. The titles and rhythmical beat continue.*

The camera then moves down to pick up Charlton Heston and Janet Leigh as they walk along the street next to the car, which is just passing them. The car reaches them and turns a corner as they do. It continues on ahead of them (out of screen space). As the camera continues to track back, *Leigh and Heston talk; we are too far away to hear what they say.* Their dress helps to communicate the period portrayed by the film—that of the mid-twentieth century.

People flash by at a quick pace, passing close to the camera. They appear in screen space suddenly, with no preparation for their entrance, and they disappear just as suddenly.

At this point in the shot, we do not yet have our bearings. We know that the car that carries the bomb is ahead, but we do not know who Leigh and Heston are or where they are going. Whatever unity there is has been provided by the all-seeing camera.

The credits continue. The camera pulls back *at their end to give a longer view of Leigh and Heston. The music dies down as we hear the first dialogue in the film, a voice from outside the frame asking, "Are you folks American citizens?" We see that the voice belongs to a man who is gradually appearing in the frame. Heston talks to him. It becomes clear that the man is a border guard and that he recognizes*

Heston as a narcotics investigator. The border guard's partner asks Heston if he is "hot on the trail of another dope ring." Leigh is identified as Heston's wife.

The car has pulled up to the border. The occupants are in the background of the action, while the prime objects of interest are Leigh and Heston as they converse with the border guards. The woman in the car is not responsive to the border guard's questions regarding her citizenship. Instead, she says that she "has a ticking noise in her head." The car is let through the border crossing.

Leigh and Heston can be seen walking toward the border as the car pulls away. Uniformed officers come toward us through screen space, passing close by the camera as they disappear off screen.

The rhythmic beat continues. People continue to flash by the camera unexpectedly and abruptly disappear. Leigh's remark, "Do you know that this is the first time that we have been together in my country?" conveys the information that it is the U.S. border that has been crossed. At this point, the movement of the camera coincides with the movement of Leigh and Heston as Heston says, "Do you realize that I haven't kissed you in over an hour?" Just as they embrace, there is the sound of an explosion. They look screen-left out of the frame *toward the source of the offscreen explosion.*

Touch of Evil, *1957*

cinema
affect

"It is one thing to say what an aesthetic object *is;* it is another thing to say what it *does* to us."[1]

This remark, typical of a popular viewpoint about the nature of film, presupposes that all judgments about a film are to be made by reference to its visual or auditory qualities only, and that one's response to a film—to its unity or disunity, humor or lack of it, to its other aesthetic elements—is irrelevant. The feelings aroused by a motion picture have nothing to do with what the motion picture is. So goes this typical conception, which neglects crucial aspects of film.

Film, as any art, has the capacity to *affect* audiences. Affects are responses to a stimulus: Viewers of a movie can have a *sense* or *impression* of something in the movie (for example, of things being distorted); they can *feel* alienated from (or involved in) the action; they can have an *emotion* about a development in the story; they can *react* by identify-

[1] Monroe Beardsley, *Aesthetics* (New York: Harcourt Brace Jovanovich, 1958), p. 34.

ing with a character. To put ourselves in contact with the aesthetic qualities of a film, we will have to take these affects into account.

This chapter deals with the affects of film and with the argument that a description of a film is incomplete without reference to them.

Film Space and Affect

The concern here will be with the ways in which onscreen space affects the viewer.

Onscreen space is both two- and three-dimensional.[2] Its two-dimensional character is, of course, derivative from the fact that film images are projected onto a flat (two-dimensional) surface. Thus, every film picture can be viewed like a painting, with design on a two-dimensional surface being the substance of what the viewer experiences. Some filmmakers attempt to emphasize the two-dimensional aspect, creating fascinating compositions on the plane of the screen and calling our attention to them.

Most filmmakers set out to create an illusion of reality. To accomplish this, they place objects and stage action within the frame in ways aimed at giving qualities of depth to onscreen space; the illusion can be quite effective. When the camera tracks through a locale, viewers have feelings much like those they have when they walk through a locale themselves (though only vision and hearing operate in perception of film space, while in perception of real-life space kinesthetic awareness plays a role as well). When the camera is stationary, the film will show objects as being either in front of or behind another object, at a distance from or close to the viewer, or with other such characteristics of everyday perception of space.

Onscreen space can be manipulated in terms of location (where objects or people are in the landscape that we see before us on the screen), distance and direction (of these objects from one another), extent, (the area objects occupy within the frame), and volume (the size and shape of objects on the screen). Using these, filmmakers often create film images that have both two- and three-dimensional qualities. In fact, many of the most powerful effects in film involve an interplay between flatness and depth. An action that both forms a design on the two-dimensional surface and is a convincing movement in the apparent depth of the screen offers a richer experience than one limited to only one of the two spatial systems (either two- or three-dimensional).

How affects are engendered is illustrated in the following analyses of portions of four films.

---

[2] See Alexander Sesonske, "Cinema Space." In David Carr and Edward S. Casey, eds., *Explorations in Phenomenology,* No. 4 (The Hague: Martinus Nijhoff, 1973), pp. 399–409.

Boudu Saved from Drowning, *1932*

Boudu Saved from Drowning

In Jean Renoir's *Boudu Saved from Drowning* (1932) Boudu, the natural man, attempts suicide by jumping into the Seine from a Paris bridge. A man who epitomizes the civilized life jumps in to save him. As he swims out to where Boudu is floundering, the camera follows in a way that takes the audience into the center of the action. However, just as the man is about to reach Boudu, there is a radical shift in camera position to a far-off perspective, which has a stunning affect on the audience's sense of space. Early shots of the rescue scene are from the bank of the river, a shooting angle from which the river looks narrow—a thin strand in screen space. The actual rescue is shown from a far-off camera position over the prow of a ship cruising in midriver, which makes for a perspective—the river dominating screen space—that gives the audience a startling sense of the river's immensity. Furthermore, the cut from the center of the action (the rescue) to the long shot (up river) leaves an expectant audience straining to see the rescue, now so far-off.

The sense of immensity experienced by the audience has a function relative to the shots that follow the rescue. Once Boudu is brought ashore, space becomes constricted. As he is carried into the rescuer's house, the actors can barely edge by the camera. Inside the house, the audience's sense of confinement is further augmented. Everything is crowded, cramped, and cluttered,

49

Boudu Saved from Drowning, *1932*

with the camera close to the action. The audience now has a sense of the contrast between the spatial qualities of two environments: on the one hand, the natural, open setting of the river; on the other, the civilized, confining setting of the house. A central meaning of the film is thus communicated— Boudu, the natural man, at home in the simple life of the open road, cannot live in the confining space of civilization.

Near the end of the film, just before Boudu returns to a life in nature, two shots again give the audience a feeling for the vastness of the space he needs. The first shot initially contains no action as the camera pans over a stream. Then from the right side of the frame, a boat appears carrying Boudu, who is embracing a maid from the house he was taken to after the rescue. Also in the boat is the man who rescued Boudu, his wife, and a rower. Boudu manages, in his inimitable way, to capsize the boat. The second shot shows his hat floating on the water. After this, no action is shown. The audience's attention during these shots is left to focus on the qualities of the natural setting. The camera is expressive of Boudu's return to a space in which he can live.

The Third Man

In Carol Reed's *The Third Man* (1949) a feeling of unease is created through the constant use of tilted framing. Throughout the film, shooting angle works in conjunction with this tilted framing, with downward and upward angles predominating. Other visual elements—such as constant background changes and much cutting into scenes in which action is underway—augment the framing and the shooting angles in creating an uneasy feeling in the viewer about the film's environment.

Sound-editing supports the mood created by the film's visual elements. The landlady's voice echoes in the halls as investigators talk to the character played by Valli. The sound is confusing and irritating. Ever-present background music, played on the zither, carries this confusing, irritating quality into the shots that follow.

At the end, when Harry Lime is trying to escape through the sewers of the city, these sounds are repeated. The voices of his pursuers echo everywhere about the sewer. Harry doesn't know where they are; hence, he doesn't know in what direction to flee. We have come to expect things to be awry in this space, and so we empathize all the more with Lime's reaction to the sounds.

Sherlock, Jr.

The empathy elicited from the audience by *The Third Man* serves to make that film more believable. If something is done that positively prevents empathy with a character, it can contribute to comedy.

In Buster Keaton's *Sherlock Jr.* (1924) Keaton is a movie projectionist who falls asleep at the controls. He dreams that he is a projectionist who leaves his place beside the movie projector to take a seat in the theatre. After watching the film for a while, he walks up to the screen area and then enters the movie itself. Most audiences, taken aback at an action so contrary to reality, will laugh as Keaton participates in the situations in the film within the film.

The impact of this scene is connected with the audience's relationship to screen space. As they sit in the space of the theatre, moviegoers perceive another space—that of the movie they watch. They are always (though usually marginally) aware of being in an everyday, three-dimensional space in the movie house. The viewer's attention, however, is focused on the changing space of the movie, and his eye identifies with the eye of the camera as it moves through the film space. He has feelings and sensations that he would have were he actually moving through such a space.

The moviegoer retains (again marginally) an awareness that one cannot go from where one is to where the events of the movie are happening; there is no space *between* the two spaces—of the film and of the viewer's presence in the theatre—that one can cross. Our recognition that what we perceive before us is "only a movie" is based upon just such basic kinds of awareness.

When Keaton performs his impossible crossing of that nonexistent space between us and the movie, we have a vivid sense of the absurdity of the situation and we are shocked by this challenge to our belief about our relationship to movie space; this is the basis of the resultant hilarity.

The Battle of Algiers, First Love, and Vivre Sa Vie

In an early sequence of Pontecorvo's *The Battle of Algiers* (see pages 3–4) as Ali, leader of the revolutionaries, is taken away by police, his background is described in a voice-over narration. Visually, the sequence creates (by use of a

Vivre Sa Vie, *1962*

kind of "bouncing" image) a sense of spatial dislocation. With its sense of location inhibited, the audience's attention tends to focus on the narration.

A similar device is used for a different reason in Maximilian Schell's first directorial effort, *First Love* (1971), early portions of which are aimed at involving the audience in the details of its old-style Russian setting. During a discussion about the nature of freedom, the action is shot at an upward angle against a blank sky. Again, as in *The Battle of Algiers,* the audience loses its sense of location, in this case in order to engender a mood appropriate to the abstract dialogue on freedom. A concrete setting might have clashed with the nature of the discussion, perhaps making the scene seem rather ridiculous.

It is with just this kind of effect (or, rather, its converse) in mind that Jean-Luc Godard, in his *Vivre Sa Vie* (1962), shoots a discussion between a prostitute and a philosopher in a café. The everyday paraphernalia—dishes, tables, waiters—of the café conspire to deflate the discussion of grand ideas.

Film Time and Affect

Time in a film—conveyed by the order and pace with which images, events, and actions succeed one another—is of three kinds: *dramatic* time, *physical* time, and *affective* time.

Dramatic time is structured by the demands of plot, characterization, theme, and other features of story development. Events of very large scope, such as the Napoleonic War against Russia, can be portrayed via dramatic time in no more than a few hours—as in the several versions of *War and Peace.* Typically, when an event is represented in terms of dramatic time, much is omitted. A viewer need not see all phases of an action in order to identify it or for it to form part of an aesthetically satisfying whole.

When a film attempts to show *all* phases of events, another time order is introduced, namely physical time. Very few films are structured entirely according to physical time. *Cleo from 5 to 7* (Agnès Varda, 1962) is a notable example of one that is. It gives a two-hour account of two hours in the life of a woman on a certain day—nothing more, nothing less. Physical time, then, refers to a filmic structuring of events at the same rate at which they would occur in the world outside the movies.

In affective time, events are ordered so as to have certain affects upon the audience's subjective sense of time. Thus, some scenes—depending on the order and pace of events—will be made to seem slow moving, others to fly by.

Incident at Owl Creek

The impact of Robert Enrico's *Incident at Owl Creek* (1962) depends on the interaction of the three types of time noted above.

As the film begins, preparations are being made for an execution by hanging on a railroad bridge high above a river. The various rituals and chores involved proceed according to physical time in that all the action is shown, including a rather long wait for the sun to rise.

When the trap is sprung and the hero is falling to his death, the rope breaks and he hurtles into the water below, where he struggles out of his bonds. These events continue the pattern of physical-time portrayal. However, they take so long that the viewer begins to feel that the man will not escape.

The protagonist comes to the surface and there follows a lyrical section expressive of the joy of simply being alive. This causes the audience to shift its way of relating to the film—from one in which it is seen as a portrayal of a man trying to escape execution to a view of it as a nonrealistic, poetic treatment of an escape. Dramatic time, therefore, becomes the dominant mode.

A remarkable shift in time then occurs. A cut is made to the execution squad back on the hill. Their attempts to mount a pursuit after the escapee are depicted in slow motion. The move into slow motion at this juncture in the story has the effect of obliterating the audience's sense of time. They now can consider the possibility that the escapee did move fast enough to get away after all.

The audience's sense of the relationship of the condemned man to his pursuers is now shattered. His too-slow-to-be-plausible escape is now matched by slow-motion pursuit. At the end of the film, many viewers are surprised by the revelation that the escape was nothing more than a wish-fulfillment fantasy. The audience begins to be deceived by this film when its sense of time is obliterated.

The audience's response to the discovery of the unreality of the escape is also prepared for by the affective time of *Incident at Owl Creek.* As the man approaches his home, not only do gates open of their own accord but his movements toward his wife are shown in overlap. The conspicuous artificiality of these representations breaks the realistic cast that marks most of his escape. Just as the man reaches his wife, his head jerks back and a cut is made to a shot of him hanging from the bridge.

Though viewers probably feel deceived, they may also feel aesthetic satisfaction. The artificiality of the magically opening gates and the overlap prepared them for the realization that the escape episode was unreal. With these preparations, a film that might have seemed a trick evokes a sense of fittingness.

Other features of the escape episode work with time to make it believable. Just as the man reaches rapids that will speed his escape, the camera makes a 360-degree turn while focusing on tree tops. The circular pattern described matches those of the rapids. As the man reaches shore, filters are used that give a thin, washed-out appearance to the environment, expressing the shock that the hero feels at the realization that he has escaped. As he runs through the forest, the camera seems to lead him on as it backtracks ahead of him. A tree-lined road becomes the frame for a shot that confers a distinctive personality on the camera: Struggling down a road, the man falls, and the camera "gives up" on him, moving down the road a distance to "wait" there for him to rise and start his desperate run anew.

All these features give an expressionistic cast to the portrayal of the man's escape. Working in conjunction with time, they leave the audience unsure how to regard it.

Hiroshima Mon Amour

Alain Resnais' *Hiroshima Mon Amour* (1959) begins with many powerful images. Shots of parts of bodies give way to sights of nuclear devastation that, in turn, give way to views of sexual embrace. The sights of nuclear destruction are horrifying; the views of physical love indistinct. The audience cannot understand what connection is being made between love, beauty, sex, parts of bodies, destruction, and the atomic bomb.

As the film progresses, the man (who is Japanese and is called Hiroshima) constantly reminds the woman (known only as Nevers, after her home town in France) that she will forget the things that ought to matter the most. She will forget the nuclear destruction; she will forget the humiliation she suffered because of her love affair with a German during World War II.

This theme of man's propensity to forget the important things is reiterated at every turn in the film. Yet in the very experiencing of the film, the viewer

Hiroshima Mon Amour, *1959*

undergoes a similar process of forgetfulness, as the film repeatedly replaces in audience consciousness the initially powerful images with others. By the time the film has ended, the vivid sense of those initially powerful images is gone. This affect on the audience is temporal in nature, for it has to do with the succession of something in the film—in this case, with the succession of images. Thus, those initial images are there not only because they fit aesthetically with the shots that follow but also because they give the audience the experience of forgetting.

Citizen Kane

Like *Hiroshima Mon Amour,* Welles' *Citizen Kane* (see pages 40–43) has an affective-time dimension that emphasizes its meaning.

Three time patterns are found in the film. The first pattern, the present, runs throughout the film. The reporter, Thompson, conducts a search in the present for hidden facts about Charles Foster Kane. Thompson's explorations take him to Kane's close associates at the newspaper, Bernstein and Leland; to his second wife, Susan Alexander; to the records of his guardian, J. Walter Thatcher; and to his butler, Raymond. Through their reminiscences about Kane, Time Pattern 2 is introduced—that of the past. Pattern 3 also consists of a recounting of past events in Kane's life, but differs from Pattern 2 in that it breaks the normal direction of the flow of events from past to present, putting the audience back in time to begin another, different subjective account of Kane. It jars the audience's involvement, forcing it to question the truth of what has already been portrayed. A Time Pattern 3 always becomes a Pattern 2. This new Pattern 2 is subsequently interrupted by a new Pattern 3, and so forth.

An example of how a Pattern 3 interrupts a Pattern 2 follows: In a Pattern 2 progression—established via reporter Thompson's reading of the Thatcher records—one first sees Kane as a boy with his parents and wealthy guardian-to-be, J. Walter Thatcher. Next he is perhaps a year older, receiving a sled at Christmas time in Thatcher's home. Then he is a young man running a newspaper. Kane finally appears as a much older man liquidating his interests in the newspaper. At this point, the normal form and progression is interrupted by a Pattern 3 sequence: Bernstein's recollections of Kane, which begin with Kane's first day at the newspaper—an event that occurred much earlier than the point where the Thatcher records leave the viewer.

The Pattern 3 sequence, juxtaposing the early Kane with the mature Kane (of a closing Pattern 2 sequence), serves to emphasize the dual nature of his life: at once an active, powerful man and an ineffective, unhappy man with a flawed private life. (This duality was part of the stereotype about the successful American man of the time.)[3]

In determining what the film portrays, the time interruptions and their affects deserve much attention. Time structuring is what permits us to see Kane's many-sided nature: Each time we think we know the man, a different subjective view of him is presented.

Sanjuro

Akira Kurosawa's *Sanjuro* (1962) ends with a samurai showdown fight that has implications for the nature of time in film. The two participants—Sanjuro (Toshiro Mifune) and Hanbei (Tatsuya Nakadai)—face each other with their swords in their scabbards, their hands slowly and surely moving to the ready position. An unusually long time passes before the swordsmen draw and strike, but when they do, the action is so fast that it can hardly be seen. Sanjuro strikes one blow, and Hanbei falls slowly to the ground. In actuality, Mifune moves his sword from the drawn position directly to a point at the side of and beyond Nakadai. An attempt to simulate a blow would have involved (as do many such sword fights) an intermediate move seeming to pass through Nakadai. In this case, however, our imagination supplies the missing step.

The background music is quite supportive of this affect, its spine-tingling sound distracting us, as does the above-mentioned wait before the fatal blow.

Because much of *Sanjuro* is a parody of the samurai genre, it may be that the missing step in Mifune's attack is omitted in a parodic spirit.

Strangers on a Train

Hitchcock's *Strangers on a Train* (1951) exemplifies both expanded and contracted time. In the film, Bruno (Robert Walker) aims to frame Guy (Farley Granger) for a crime that he himself committed. To do this he must plant a piece of evidence (a cigarette lighter) on a certain island. Bruno sets out for the island, but Guy, though suspecting Bruno's intentions, cannot follow him until

---

[3] Norman Gambill, *An Art Historical Perspective on Citizen Kane* (Syracuse, Syracuse University Ph.D. dissertation, 1976).

Sanjuro, *1962*

he completes a tennis match. Much tension results from cutting back and forth between Guy's tennis match and Bruno's movements, which include his bus trip to the island, his temporary loss of the lighter, and his subsequent wait there. The suspense is also heightened by the constant reminder, provided by the editing, of what awaits Guy on the island after the match is completed.

The trips to the island have a most unusual character: Bruno's (while Guy is stymied by the tennis match) seems endless; Guy's swift. The oddness of this chase is perhaps best described as a time-warp. By devoting much footage to them, both Bruno's movements to the island and Guy's tennis match are, in effect, expanded; time is contracted during Guy's movement to the island.

The Birds

In Hitchcock's *The Birds* (1963) great flocks of birds gather in a small town and attack the residents. The attack scenes, which mount in intensity through the film, are interrupted roughly at the midpoint of the film by a straightforward scene in a village coffee shop. In an interview with Hitchcock, François Truffaut raised questions about the length and "appropriateness" of the scene that are really questions about *intensity* and about *unity*. If the café scene is too long, then *The Birds* loses intensity; if it does not fit with the action, then the film tends to lose unity.

Hitchcock's reply focused on audience response. He admitted that the scene in the village café did not add to the story, but he explained:

> . . . I felt that after the attack of the birds on the children at the birthday party, the small birds coming down the chimney, and the attack of the crows outside the school, we should *give the audience a rest* [Italics mine—Au.] before going back to the horror. . . . That scene in the restaurant is a breather that allows for a few laughs. The character of the drunk is straight out of an O'Casey play, and the elderly lady ornithologist is pretty interesting. In truth, you are right. The scene is a little on the long side, but I feel that if the audience is absorbed in it, it is automatically shortened. . . . I've always measured the length or brevity of a scene by the degree of interest it holds for the public. If they're completely absorbed, it's a short scene; if they're bored, the scene is bound to be too long.[4]

These observations by Hitchcock bring out the *relational* charactor of both intensity and unity. Contrary to the traditional view, intensity and unity are qualities not of the film per se but of the relation between what is perceived on the screen and what takes place in the viewers—namely, what feelings they have and how they relate to what they perceive (for example, being absorbed in the café scene).

According to Hitchcock's interpretation of the village café scene, it contributes both to the intensity and to the unity of *The Birds*. Giving the audience a

---

[4] François Truffaut, *Hitchcock* (New York: Simon and Schuster, 1967), p. 221.

"rest" from the horror sharpens the impact of subsequent horrifying events. Thus the café scene contributes to the intensity of *The Birds*. It contributes to the unity of the film by its capacity to absorb the audience in its action.

North by Northwest

In Hitchcock's *North by Northwest* (1959) the hero (Cary Grant) has a conversation that sums up what has happened to him during the first third of the film. The deafening sound of airplanes (the scene is at an airport) drowns out most of the dialogue, but enough is heard for the audience to realize that the bizarre events that have befallen Grant are being summarized. The episode takes only about thirty seconds, while an actual recounting of the events would take at least three minutes. This affect is called *temporal dislocation*. Since the scene seems unreal, the audience is dislocated from the time order of the film at this point.

Most Hollywood films of the 1930s, 40s, and 50s enhanced audience involvement by conscientiously "locating" the audience in a film's space and time. Various means were used: A three-dimensional look very much like the three-dimensional space we live in every day was cultivated through the careful arrangement of objects, actors, and sets, and careful attention to the quality and succession of events in a film gave the time order the coherence of ordinary, everyday life. It is this sense of being located in the time of the film that is thwarted in the airport scene from *North by Northwest*.

Aesthetically the dislocation affect serves a most important unifying function. Dislocation fits the bizarre story line of the film. It would be inappropriate to have the audience located in the film's time when its content is so bizarre, and so it is better to transport the audience *out* of time. Hitchcock would not want the audience to feel at home with the strange events that befall Grant.[5]

Unity in *North by Northwest* turns out to be a relation between the film and the audience rather than a visual or sound quality of the film itself. The relation is between what the audience perceives (a bizarre story) and what they have a sense of (being dislocated from the time of the film).

Conclusion

One popular view about the nature of the motion picture medium is that it is nothing more than the sum of its visual and sound qualities, and that aesthetic judgments about a film can be based solely on what can be seen and heard during a screening of the film. An advocate of this view may take the position that statements about the affects of a film can be reduced entirely to state-

[5] Ibid., p. 191.

ments about the visual and/or sound qualities of the film, the argument being that when the viewer is absorbed, dislocated, or otherwise affected, there must be some visual or sound feature of the film that elicits the response.

However, in order to identify what affects a film has, one must know the perceptual abilities of the audience. These are independent of what is perceivable in the film, and thus cinema's affects are powers that a film has that go beyond its visual and sound qualities.[6]

Another popular view about film restricts what film is even more, saying that it is a primarily visual medium. Our foregoing analysis of the relation of sound to the affective qualities of the motion picture indicates that no such generalization is correct. In the space and time illustrations of this chapter, analysis of the aesthetic qualities of the scenes discussed depended on all three aspects of the medium (visual, aural, and affective), with no one having primacy. To argue that a film will not work aesthetically unless it has good visual elements is true but irrelevant. The fact that a necessary condition for aesthetic qualities in film is the presence of well-designed visual elements does not mean that any particular aesthetic quality is produced primarily by one or more visual element. In other words, a film will no doubt be flat, uninteresting, and uninvolving if it has no interesting visual elements, but when a film does have aesthetic qualities, visual elements need not be the primary factor at work.

---

[6] The distinction here is between what are called "occurrent" and "dispositional" properties. Visual and sound qualities are occurrent properties. Affective qualities are dispositional; dispositional properties are by definition unperceivable.

audience
capacities

In films, as in most things, our expectations play an important role in what we perceive. The following discussion of the filmmaking style of Jean-Luc Godard takes the position that the aesthetic effects he achieves are in part dependent on the expectations of his audience and that these expectations, in turn, are partly a product of the times during which a film is experienced. This time-relative status illustrates two things: Part of what a film is is determined by the times in which it is exhibited, and some of the aesthetic qualities of a film will differ as audiences differ.

Exploiting Expectation

Dislocation

In the Films of Godard   Through much of the 1960s, Jean-Luc Godard was engaged in creating a cinematic equivalent to the Brechtian alienation in the theatre. Brecht felt that neither audience nor director should view a play as escape or catharsis; hence, the audience had to be alienated from the dramatic action of the play. Brecht did not want the audience to leave the play's social commentary behind in the theatre. He wanted it to have an effect on how the playgoer lived from then on.

The Godard equivalent of Brechtian alienation is *dislocation,* and Godard marshals all of the considerable resources of the cinematic medium toward the end of dislocating his audience spatially, temporally, and dramatically.

Up to the time Godard's first major film, *Breathless* (1959), appeared, the dominant thrust of filmic expression had been toward transporting the audience into the space, time, and dramatic center of the film. Films were often praised for their ability to transport us out of our everyday lives into the worlds of action, romance, suspense, drama, the incongruous, and the sublime. The Hollywood cameras of Hawks, Ford, Hitchcock, and Donen carved out the space of the film's action. They provided three-dimensionality and made filmic space look like the familiar space of our lives. Stories had beginnings, middles, and ends, dramatic reversals, climaxes, and, most of all, well-motivated characterizations and attractive stars.

Godard reacted against all of this. He developed new techniques to transport the audience *out* of the space, time, and dramatic action of his films. Godard's camera does not move into the space of the film. Instead, it circles about outside the space, moving around its objects, not in among them. Space in Godard's films is often flat, shallow, and constricted.

Godard uses color in ways contrary to the notions associated with the painter's means of conveying depth by putting the brightest colors in the foreground, with the values of others gradually diminishing with recession into the distance or background.

Godard reverses this process in *Vivre Sa Vie* (1962) and *La Chinoise* (1967). In the black-and-white film *Vivre Sa Vie,* he repeatedly places actors against monochromatic walls with the camera close. The spectator sees little space in front of the actors, and the walls in the background tend to preclude any sense of depth.

In *La Chinoise* Godard has a young band of would-be revolutionaries repaint the building (that will house their Communist cell) a uniform red that stares out at us and defeats our attempts to perceive depth. Weaker-colored objects that move about in front of this dominating background combine with it to give the film space a look that does not conform with the space we ordinarily live in.

Vivre Sa Vie, *1962*

La Chinoise, *1967*

Mirrors are used in an interesting way to distort space in *Vivre Sa Vie* and *A Married Woman* (1964). In these films, they act in concert with a static camera to give the viewer a sense of rebounding from the space.

Thus Godard aims to achieve a space that is distorted, shallow, uneasy, and uninvolving, so that spectators will be expelled from it—dislocated, transported out. So placed, we will be better able to contemplate a film's ideas, grasp its portrayal of reality, understand its social commentary, and, most important, apply its message to our everyday lives.

Some further aspects of Godard's use of spatial dislocation are exemplified in the opening sequences from the black-and-white film *Alphaville* (1965). In these sequences, Godard introduces many elements that have a high graphic content—such as posters, backdrops, arrows, flashing lights, and murals. These elements serve to focus our attention on the two-dimensional aspects of what we see in the screen space. Godard's shooting angle and object movement further discourage conventional involvement. The former avoids action that moves either directly away from or directly toward the camera (called *shooting along the axis of the lens*); such action tends to involve us much more than that along a line at right angles to the axis. Nonaxial shooting also gives a relatively flat look to space; objects and people tending to appear as if all were moving in a single plane.

In *Alphaville* Godard plays with our expectations—expectations derived from our previous film experience. On multiple levels, he parodies the genres of the gangster movie, science fiction, and the antiutopian nightmare, as well as the documentary about urban settings. These parodies prevent our involvement with what we witness on the screen because they evoke a rather high degree of emotional distance.

Godard also makes stylistic references to previous films—references which remind us that we are "just watching a movie." From the time Lemmie Caution (the protagonist) enters the hotel in the city of Alphaville until the time he reaches his room, there is only one shot. This long take is in part a reference to other famous instances of long, unedited sequences—to F.W. Murnau's *Sunrise* (1927), for example, and also the previously discussed opening of Welles' *Touch of Evil* (pages 43–46). This long take differs from the shots it calls to mind, however, in that it dislocates the audience from the object of greatest interest. Pillars, posts, elevator walls, and darkness come between us and Lemmie Caution as he checks in at the hotel and as he walks with the staff seductress to his room. These intervening objects act like cuts in the long take and serve to lessen our awareness of its length. More important, they limit our sense of a character moving through a clearly identifiable space.

A further indication that what we are seeing is just a movie is the camera style throughout the opening sequences. Highly autonomous, independent of the action, the camera precedes Lemmie Caution and is often at a location before him. Because our attention is drawn to the camera, we have diffculty becoming involved.

Finally, lighting helps to form our perception of the world of *Alphaville.* All visual artists have to make a fundamental choice about the status of light in the world of their work. Is the world to be that of darkness or light? Rembrandt portrays an essentially dark world where light enters only in an accidental way. Bergman's *The Seventh Seal* (1956) opens in darkness and its "feel" remains predominantly that of a dark world. By contrast, all of the sequences of Jacques Demy's *The Young Girls of Rochefort* (1967) occur in bright, daytime settings. Demy's world for *Rochefort* is essentially one of light. In *Alphaville,* a dark world is created; light appears largely in isolated pools.

As mentioned above, *Breathless* was Godard's first major attempt to reject the popular film of the day. In it he introduced the three modes of dislocation that would become his trademark.

Spatial dislocation is brought about primarily by the gradual creation of an unconventional spatial geography. In conventional treatments, a car that is first shown moving screen-right will continue this screen-right movement in subsequent shots unless some motivation for a countermovement is established. Similarly, in a conventional cut from a long shot to a close-up, the location of elements in the space will remain constant. For example, three men seen in a long shot will, in a following close-up, be in the same position relative to each other—unless some movement out of that position was indicated before the cut.

In the murder sequence in *Breathless,* Godard systematically thwarts any effort the audience may make to establish spatial coherence. Just as a marked movement of Belmondo's car to screen-right is established, a violent cut to his car screeching screen-left is made. No sooner are we getting comfortable with Belmondo's point of view inside his car, than Godard's camera thrusts us to a fixed point *outside* the car at tire-tread level as the car continues by, leaving us behind.

Godard's method for temporal dislocation turns, again, upon reversal of a well-developed technique of the conventional film. Central to creating a convincing time order (if viewing time is not to correspond to dramatic time) is the necessity of giving the spectator a sense of having experienced a *whole* event, while having seen only portions of it. Godard often gives less of an event than is needed to achieve this sense of wholeness. Again in the murder sequence, jump cuts (which leave out part of an action) are used so that rather than flowing forward, the action "jumps," providing too little information to give us the feel of events in everyday life. As with Godard's film space, the time order is one with which we can feel neither comfortable nor involved.

Finally, the sequence exemplifies a kind of dramatic dislocation. As the murder scene develops, the audience sees more and more of Belmondo's character—in this case, his casualness—to respond to. While driving, he shoots at the sun, talks to himself in a brattish way, makes fun of other drivers, and comments on the countryside. But the interest in Belmondo that is aroused is never consummated, for no more is made of it. Thus, in this case, dislocation arises when dramatic conventions are not followed.

Although, in the above-mentioned murder sequence spatial and temporal dislocations abound, there remains the familiar sense—as philosopher Stanley Cavell puts it—of viewing the world while feeling unseen.[1] An instance of *dramatic* dislocation, however, disturbs this comfortable feeling by directly involving the audience in the movie itself. This occurs when Belmondo makes a comment straight at the audience.

The shot analysis that follows gives a precise idea of how Godard's technique of dislocation works.

Analysis of a Sequence from Godard's *Breathless*

SHOT 1

> *B (Belmondo) in his car on a country road. (Preceded by a long dissolve from B in his car by the river in Paris.)*

[1] Stanley Cavell, *The World Viewed* (New York: Viking Press, 1971), p. 102.

Breathless, *1959. Shot 1*

If you don't like the sea...

SHOTS 2–5

> *A series of jump cuts of varying views of B as he drives. B hums throughout.* This creates a time dislocation. The sound provides a certain amount of continuity.

SHOT 6

> *A long, traveling shot from B's viewpoint inside his car. He catches up with a car ahead.* Space is locational at this point.

SHOT 7

> *B's car proceeds in a screen-downward direction.* Here we experience spatial dislocation because earlier shots (1–6) show B's car moving upward in screen space. *There is a shift in viewpoint from inside to outside B's car.* This shot produces further spatial dislocation.

> *B passes a car, commenting, "He won't pass me in that tin crate." The camera pans back after B passes and looks back, but we see no "tin crate."* Conventionally, when a camera turns to follow the direction of a character's glance, we expect to see something. Thus, seeing nothing and being given no explanation leaves us dislocated.

SHOT 8

> *B's car travels screen-right.* Again there is spatial dislocation since the preceding shots showed B driving upward and downward in screen space. (The direction of travel becomes firmly established in this shot.) *B, talking to himself, says that he is getting away from Paris and that once he has arranged his affairs, he will "pick up the money, I'll ask Patricia yes or no, Buenas Noches, my love, and off to Genoa, Milano, Roma."* This produces a dramatic dislocation; we do not know to whom or what B is referring. *B then says, "The countryside is pretty,"* and, flamboyantly, *"I love France."* Pastoral music comes from the car radio. Here contrary elements clash with his tough manner. At this point we are engaged by B's character, but there is nothing forthcoming to allow us to satisfy our interest; hence the dramatic dislocation.

SHOT 9

> *B travels screen-left.* Again we are spatially dislocated.

SHOT 10

> *B moves screen-right.* This continues the series of spatial dislocations. *B looks directly into the camera (at the audience) and says: "If you don't like the sea and you don't care for the mountains, and you don't care for the big city, get screwed."* Thus our conventional sense of seeing the world while feeling unseen is violated, and a dislocation results. *The music becomes bouncy. As he passes two girls B slows the car, suddenly altering the pace. He says, "They both stink.*

Let them walk." Tough music resumes. B reaches for a gun in the glove compartment. He plays at firing the gun.

SHOT 11

B's car moves upward on the diagonal and to the right in screen space. He shoots at the sun, saying, as he does, "lovely sunshine." Again the audience contends with a mixture of conflicting elements. *B criticizes the other drivers, continuing his monologue.* Conveyed are his brattishness, his irritability, his impatience, and his desire to live in the moment.

B passes a policeman. Though he has stolen the car, he is unperturbed, remarking, "You should never put on the brakes; cars were meant to go."

Cars are made to go, not to stop!

Breathless, *1959. Shot 11*

SHOT 12

The front bumper of B's car, seen from so low a point that it cannot be taken to be a human point of view. (Viewpoints, until now, have been those that human observers might have.) *The turn signal of the car and the center line of the road are visible.*

SHOT 13

The dashboard of the car as B passes a truck. "Shit, the cops," exclaims B. The police are seen on the right-hand side of the road. B worries about having recklessly passed so many cars.

(The pace is extremely fast, both within and between Shots 14 through 19 and the tough-mannered music is heard throughout.)

SHOT 14

B's car moving screen-left passes another car and a truck.

SHOT 15

Inside the car, which is moving screen-right, the camera makes a 180-degree turn. The camera ends its turn. This leaves us with no sense of being inside the car. The police can be seen on their motorcycles appearing from behind the truck that B has just passed. The pace is very rapid, making it difficult to keep up with the action.

SHOT 16

Jump cut: The police behind B. Inside the car the camera turns back 180 degrees. We get our bearings again.

SHOT 17

B's car first seen from the right front passes another car. Both B's car and the car passed go by the stationary camera. This gives a powerful sense of speed. B's car moves toward screen-right.

Breathless, 1959. Shot 17

SHOT 18

    The police travel screen-left (spatial dislocation) *on their motorcycles as they pursue B. The motorcycles leave the frame, and the camera turns to follow their movements. Cut from the cycles as they are in midframe.* (This is the same place in screen space as the cut from B's car.)

Breathless, *1959. Shot 18*

SHOT 19

    B stops on a side road that slopes downward in screen space. He says, "My goose is cooked!" There are sounds of passing cars and the music. This provides continuity.

    (The pace of Shots 20 through 26 is slow enough so that action can be easily identified, contrasting with the fast pace of Shots 14 through 19.)

SHOT 20

B looks toward the main road and deliberately removes a cigarette from his mouth. His casualness is thus reemphasized.

SHOT 21

A motorcycle policeman passes on the main road.

SHOT 22

B opens the hood of his car. This provides a dislocation, since the time between this shot and Shot 20 has not been long enough for B to have done this.

SHOT 23

The second motorcycle policeman passes on the main road. B has looked in that direction, so this shot fulfills our expectations. *The second policeman continues along the main road.*

SHOT 24

B works on his car, pretending to be an innocent bystander to the chase. He looks back again at the main road.

SHOT 25

The second policeman comes down the side road toward B. At this point, spatial location has been rather firmly established.

SHOT 26

B reaches for the gun in the glove compartment of his car. In doing so, he moves to the center of the frame—the identical point in screen space into which the policeman had moved in the previous shot. In this sense, their motions (as though predestined) converge. *A shadow falls briefly across B.*

SHOT 27

From above, B's hat is seen as he faces right. We expect B to face left because Shot 26 seems to have left the policeman there. Later we realize that the policeman ran by B (the shadow in Shot 26) to take a position on B's right. *A voice says: "Don't move or I'll shoot."*

SHOT 28

A jump cut to B's forearm is followed by a pan to B's hand on the gun. B cocks the gun.

At this point there is a change from medium shots to extreme close-ups, and the sense of location becomes minimal. We are made more aware of the vertical and horizontal movements of the camera and our attention tends to focus more on the surface of the image. A further dislocation, therefore, occurs. It is not spatial or temporal and not concerned with character; rather it is systematic, for the depiction of space abruptly shifts from a three-dimensional to a two-dimensional system.

Breathless, *1959. Shot 28*

SHOT 29

> *A jump cut to the gun's cylinder as it turns, and a pan right and forward to the end of the gun barrel and beyond it.*

SHOT 30

> *The policeman falls left into the bushes, struck by B's bullet. Just before he is struck, he is seen in midscreen, precisely the position occupied by the tip of the gun barrel at the end of the preceding shot.* Thus a conjunction of the two images is established. *When the policeman falls, the camera moves so as to keep him in midscreen.* Graphically the thrust of the gun shape is horizontal; its movement, however, is vertical, establishing a tension between its three- and two-dimensional aspects.

> There is a temporal dislocation associated with this shot as well. The tilt-pan (Shot 29) over B and the gun is slow. We expect B to act fast, given the circumstances, so that this slowness makes the fateful act all the more decisive and intentional. Such an effect is appropriate, given its ultimately fatal nature (to B as well as the policeman).

SHOT 31

> *A long take follows as B flees on foot across an open field. He is kept in midscreen throughout, while music signals forthcoming disaster.*

SHOT 32

> *The camera tracks in a leisurely way over the bridge next to Nôtre Dame in Paris and then over the Seine.* The changed mood again dislocates the viewer in that expectations related to B's flight are unfulfilled.

Changes in Perception

Although Godard's early films dislocate audiences, who are used to viewing films that carefully specify space and time visually, as jump cuts become *more* common and as people lose the expectation of a coherent spatial geography, such dislocation will become *less* common. Being aware that moviegoers may become accustomed to his dislocation techniques, Godard, in his later films— *One Plus One* (1968), *Wind from the East* (1969), *Tout Va Bien* (1972)—has developed new devices for leaving his audience aware of reality in a new way and disposed to involve themselves in social causes (what Brecht called "being productively disposed").

The knowledge that perceptual capacities and expectations change with time carries an important implication. Since an audience has certain capacities and expectations and since these features of the audience vary as the movies they experience (and, hence, their experience of movies) change, it follows that qualities inherent in a film can change. *Breathless*, for instance, had a capacity to leave 1959 audiences productively disposed, but it may not have such an effect on 1999 audiences. In this sense a film can have qualities that once were seen, but are not now.

Partial Illusion

As cues of perspective and shadow help us to "see" a three-dimensional space where there is only a flat movie screen, similarly, we sometimes "see" the images of a black-and-white movie in the colors we would expect it to have.[2]

A scene in John Ford's *The Grapes of Wrath* (1939) is illustrative of how this *partial illusion* can be encouraged. After a long trip from drought-stricken Oklahoma, a migrant family marvels at the greenness of the California landscape. Though the film is in black and white, the audience too "sees" that verdant quality partly because Ford prepared it for this perception by shooting rich textures and volumes of the California landscape in a way that emphasized their contrast with the uniformly flat and dull look of dust-bowl Oklahoma— which had dominated the screen to that point.

In François Truffaut's *The Wild Child* (1970) scenes of the child in his natural environment of the forest show much texture, volume, and contrast of the kind (such as in Ford's film) that encourage illusions of color. The civilized environment is presented in smooth grays, with emphatic tones and textures largely absent. This difference fosters the partial-illusion phenomenon in the forest

---

[2] See Rudolf Arnheim, *Film as Art* (Berkeley: University of California Press, 1950), p. 68. Arnheim speculates that audiences have this capacity to experience the partial illusion of seeing color values in black-and-white films. He notes the surprising reaction that audiences often have during the live appearance of the actors at the conclusion of a premiere showing of a black-and-white film. The audience is so involved in perceiving the actors in color in black and white that the actors' normal coloring seems unrealistic.

The Wild Child, *1970*

scenes, reflecting the theme of *The Wild Child*: that life in the civilized world is less rich than in the primitive.

The partial illusion of seeing color in black-and-white movies becomes significant in view of the widespread feeling of the 40s and 50s that color movies were not "realistic." Those who so regarded color movies were for the most part viewing black-and-white movies. With their capacities for seeing color in black and white being called upon much more, it was likely that they would see the color in color movies as exaggerated.[3]

[3] The remarks in this paragraph are not to be taken as the results of experimental research, but rather as conclusions warranted by common-sense observation.

The appearance in 1971 of Peter Bogdanovich's *The Last Picture Show,* a black-and-white depiction of small-town America in the 50s, reveals much about where we have come in our relationship to color and black-and-white films. For an audience of the 70s, whose experience is largely of films in color, the use of black and white has the effect of distancing a film's events.[4]

The contemporary audience finds the reality of Anarene, Texas in *The Last Picture Show* to have a colder, duller, and more subdued quality than the reality they perceive in color movies. In the thirty years from Ford's *The Grapes of Wrath* to *The Last Picture Show* we have come full circle: Where in the 40s, color gave an unrealistic look to dramas, in the 70s black and white has become the unrealistic mode. Thus, viewer perception of color and black and white admits of an important element of relativity. How an audience views some aspect of a film is not governed only by qualities intrinsic to the thing viewed, but also by what the audience has grown accustomed to and by how its perceptual capacities have (or have not) developed.

The Factor of Belief

The phenomenon of dislocation is indicative of how aesthetic qualities can be determined by audience expectations—expectations that derive from both movie and extramovie experience. And the partial illusion of seeing color in black and white is illustrative of how *changing perceptual abilities* affect aesthetic qualities. This section will describe how *beliefs* govern some of the aesthetic qualities of films. Many of the beliefs—about love, marriage, nature, society, God, freedom, the past, the future—that we bring to the viewing of movies are held in common and originate in varied aspects of our culture; others derive directly from the movies themselves.

The presence of aesthetic qualities in a film depends in part on whether or not it makes contact with our beliefs. Mike Nichols' *The Graduate* put the audience of 1967 in touch with some of its cherished beliefs. Much of the film's humor and liveliness is produced by its relation to these beliefs. Prevailing beliefs of that time included such notions as: good wins out in the end; the younger generation can live a better life if it can reject the morality of the older; the key to success is a college education; and marriage is a must for living a fulfilled life.

The Graduate sets these beliefs in their usual thematic trappings and then undercuts them. One of the dominant themes of the love story genre (into which *The Graduate* fits) is that of the last-minute rescue of the heroine by the hero (good wins out in the end). As the story usually goes, the heroine has been

[4] Allan Casebier, "The Concept of Aesthetic Distance," *The Personalist*, Vol. 52, No. 1 (Winter 1971), pp. 70–91.

The Graduate, *1967*

brought by circumstance to the point where she is about to marry the wrong man. The hero, overcoming many obstacles and engaging in a harrowing chase, reaches the heroine just at the moment when, standing at the altar, she is about to say the fateful words. With much flurry and to the astonishment of the assembled throng, he whisks her away. Off they ride, sail, or fly to a future of happiness, secure in the realization that their reconciliation was meant to be: It was he that she and she that he really loved all along.

In Nichols' film, though there is a last-minute rescue, the hero (Ben) does not really arrive in time to rescue the heroine (Elaine Robinson). Instead he arrives after the wedding ceremony, robbing his act of its mythic sanctity. Moreover, in using a large white cross to keep the wedding party at bay and to block a door during the getaway, Ben shows a disdain for the symbols of moral authority that is at odds with the sense of "fittingness" conventionally associated with such a "rescue." Thus, Ben's transgressions undercut the expectations of those who are accustomed to movies that conform to the last-minute-rescue theme.

The alterations in the theme continue as Ben and Elaine, safely aboard a bus, stare straight ahead in a subdued mood that is quite the contrary of the happily-ever-after tone with which the theme conventionally ends.

Throughout the film, the bourgeois life of the lovers' parents is savagely parodied; the belief utilized here being one of current fashion: young people can be happy once free of their parents' life styles. Although Ben and Elaine have supposedly achieved that state, the final scene (of the two sitting on the bus) leaves us with the feeling that they may well end no happier than their parents.

The beliefs built upon in *The Graduate* exerted much the same influence on the 1967 audience that they do today. When these beliefs have less force, however, the capacities of the film to create and undercut expectations will be correspondingly diminished, and *The Graduate* will no longer seem as funny or intense.

Examination of a film from another era can help illustrate how our experience of film is often relative. Roberto Rossellini's *Paisan* (1946) struck its postwar audience as realistic, in this case because it reversed themes that had been based on prevailing beliefs. Wartime movies had promoted a romantic view of war, in which heroes of battle were glamorized, their patriotism glorified.

Paisan gives quite a different view. Depicting the American invasion of Italy, it portrays no heroes and emphasizes the harsh, cruel aspects of the war experience. It is a steady stream of poverty, urchins, drunkenness, cynicism, baseness, and brawling. *Paisan's* power is traceable to its capacity to unmake romanticisms about the war. Its audiences, anticipating a film in which a war was being fought by heroes, found themselves drawn-up short in their expectations.

The opening scene develops along standard "romantic" lines. The atmosphere is in soft focus, the moment tender. A lover lights a cigarette. This attracts the attention of a German soldier, who kills him; the woman is killed shortly thereafter. Audience expectations of romance were smashed. In a later segment, a whore picks up an American soldier. In bed, he reminisces about a meeting six months earlier with a beautiful woman, Francesca. In a flashback we see that the woman he recalls is now, unrecognized by him, the whore. While she sleeps she departs, leaving him a note telling him where to find the innocent Francesca of his memory.

In an audience of that postwar time the expectation was that the soldier would go to the place designated in the note, that Francesca, divested of her whore's clothes and manner, would appear, and they would rediscover one another. The American throws away the directions she has given him, and the segment ends with a shot of a lonely Francesca waiting for a man who will never arrive.

The beliefs that *Paisan* built upon and then reversed are no longer dominant. *Paisan* does not now have the realistic effect that it had at the time of its initial appearance. Indeed, its segments seem quite contrived. This relativity of realism is not surprising; some qualities of films change with time because part of what film art (or any other art) is, is a capacity to affect audiences of certain times. As audiences' beliefs, expectations, sensitivities, and perceptual capacities change so (for those audiences) do the qualities of a film.

cinema's powers to portray

PART
TWO

PART
TWO

PART
TWO

PAF
TW

P
T

Theories about the relation of film image to the real have had a prominent place in ideas about how film portrays its subject. In Chapter 5, three well-known theorists and their views are discussed. Chapter 6 deals with how things can be made real or unreal within the world of the film. Chapter 7 describes another kind of cinematic reality, the surreal.

the wedding of the real and art

An object, characterization, situation, action, or event in a film can strike us as real because it corresponds with our experience of the world or because it is believable in terms of the self-contained world of the specific film.

One concern of film theorists has been the relation of screen image to reality. Their inquiry has led them to ask the questions: Can a film faithfully represent the real? If a film reproduces the real, can it at the same time be art? Is it artistically desirable to create a film that represents the real?

Theories about the ideal relation of film image and the real range from those that advocate a total correspondence between the two to those that argue for their total divorcement. Three theories will be considered here that represent various positions along this continuum. The Russian filmmaker Sergei Eisenstein argued for a film style that involves a *divorce* of screen image and reality. According to the opposing view of André Bazin, a French film critic and film historian, the more artistic efforts in film have involved a close *correspondence* between screen image and reality. Bazin cites as examples films by Jean Renoir, Orson Welles, William Wyler, Robert Flaherty, Vittorio De Sica, and others. A middle course between Eisenstein and Bazin was advanced by the German psychologist Rudolf Arnheim, who advocated striving to remain faithful to physical reality while exploring the ways in which film image diverges from it.

All these theories share an *essentialist* approach, describing various features as either making a film more real or less real apart from the context in which they occur, apart from the differences among audiences that experience the film, and apart from other such *relativist* factors.

In line with this shared essentialist approach, a determination of how well a part or all of a film exemplifies reality is made by measuring these *reality-making* and *unreality-making* features against one another. The more dominant the reality-making features, the more real the film, and vice versa.

Eisenstein's Montage Style

Sergei Eisenstein and other early Russian filmmakers developed the *montage style* in order to achieve a divorcement of screen image and reality.[1] "Montage" refers to the connecting of individual shots so that they relate to compose a meaningful whole.

According to Eisenstein, the unedited fragments captured by the camera possess neither meaning nor aesthetic quality until they are connected according to montage principles, when the result becomes a vehicle for communicating socially and artistically significant visions.

Eisenstein draws analogies between film and music and poetry to justify placing so much emphasis on editing rather than photography. No single note of music or single word of poetry (his argument goes) has meaning or artistic quality; it is the same with a single shot in film.

An experiment by another Russian director, Lev Kuleshov, is illustrative of montage method and of why a single shot may not be regarded as meaningful. In this experiment, a shot of an actor's face is used in two different contexts with strikingly different results. In the first shot series, a starving prisoner is given a bowl of soup. His face appears to express wonderful happiness; he devours the soup. In the second shot series, the prisoner longs for freedom, for birds, for sun. The door is opened and we see his reaction to the sun. Although Kuleshov used the very same shot of the prisoner's reaction in both montages, to the viewer his expression looks different. As Kuleshov points out:

> . . . The spectator himself completes the connected shots and sees in it what has been suggested to him by the montage.[2]

---

[1] Most notable among the other Russian montagists were V. I. Pudovkin and Lev Kuleshov.
[2] Jay Leyda, *Kino: A History of the Russian and Soviet Film* (London: Allen and Unwin, 1960), p. 165.

Alfred Hitchcock created his own version of the Kuleshov experiment in his film *Rear Window* (1953). Hitchcock's (in his words) developed as follows:

> . . . Let's take a close-up of Stewart looking out the window at a little dog that's being lowered in a basket. Back to Stewart, who has a kindly smile. But if in the place of the little dog you show a half-naked girl exercising in front of her open window, and you go back to a smiling Stewart again, this time he's seen as a dirty old man![3]

The shots within each of the above-mentioned sequences are of different times and places. Severing these objects and appearances from their everyday space and time connections and uniting them in a certain way allows for the creation of concepts not inherent in the unedited film fragment (the shot), with its "factual immutability."[4]

Eisenstein's view that cultural conditioning often inhibits perception[5] is reflected in his *October* (1928), in which a montage helps convey a specific but perhaps unperceived aspect of Kerensky, the man who led the provisional government prior to the October Revolution. Shots of a uniformed Kerensky are intercut with views of a peacock with its plumage in full display. Since the peacock and Kerensky are not located in the same time and space, our attention seeks other ways to connect the look and actions of bird and leader. The desired connection is found in the concept of *display*—by a leader (Kerensky) and a peacock. Thus we are taken out of our ordinary way of perceiving authority.

Eisenstein saw *conflict* between shots as one of the bases of art in film.[6] Many of the artistic potentials of conflict as used by Eisenstein were illustrated in the discussion of editing in Chapter 1. In *October, scale* expresses conflict in a scene where a crowd of relatively tiny people are shown pulling down a giant statue that symbolizes an opposed regime (see page 28). The "Odessa Steps" sequence from *Potemkin* illustrates many of the other forms of conflict. *Graphic qualities* conflict when the troops march against the people running down the steps. The ordered, relentless movements of the soldiers form graphic patterns that conflict with the fragmented patterns created by the people as they scatter. *Shadow and light* conflict when the woman carries her injured child under the shadows (symbolizing the soldiers' power over her) cast by the advancing soldiers. Conflict of *an event and the time it takes to occur* is at work in the "Steps" sequence as a whole: The enormity of the event is in conflict with the relatively short time it takes to happen. Conflict of *volumes* is evident in the sequence in which hundreds of tiny boats welcome the massive battleship to port.

No doubt a host of other examples from scenes in Eisenstein's work illustrate conflict. His films are filled with editing based upon this dialectic form.

---

[3] François Truffaut, *Hitchcock* (New York: Simon and Schuster, 1967), p. 159.
[4] Sergei Eisenstein, *Film Form* (New York: Meridian Books, 1963), p. 5.
[5] Ibid., p. 35. Eisenstein goes so far as to say that "absolute realism is by no means the correct form of perception. It is simply the function of a certain form of social structure."
[6] Ibid., pp. 37–41, 48–56. For descriptions of conflict forms.

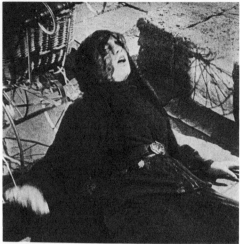

The Battleship Potemkin, *1925*

The point should be clear, however, that individual shots are not thought to be artistic or meaningful in themselves but only in their connection with others, via some structure of conflict. Much emphasis, therefore, is placed—in Eisenstein's theory about the relation (or divorcement) of film image and the real—on editing rather than on photography.

Bazin's Long-take Style

By contrast with Eisenstein, André Bazin emphasizes the photographic basis of the motion picture. For him there is much meaning and artistic value within a single shot. Though editing plays a vital role in the art film, it is not to be thought of as the primary vehicle. In Bazin's view, the meaningful and artistic cinematic style is that employing *long take and deep focus.*

This style is one most often used when situations and actions are photographed. Ideally the long take captures a complete action within a single shot. Editing, then, serves the function of connecting complete actions, each with meaning and artistic qualities of its own.

Bazin's reference to a complete action as the substance photographed in a long take has its source in the theories of Aristotle, who contends that artistic drama portrays a complete action, which has a beginning (what follows nothing by causal necessity but is followed naturally); an end (what naturally follows but has nothing following it); and a middle (what follows as other elements follow it).[7]

The opening shot in Orson Welles' *Touch of Evil* (pages 43–46) is an example of a complete action. The setting and placing of the time bomb in the car is the beginning of the action. The process started by the bomber's action is then developed in a shot that intertwines the actions of Heston, Leigh, and the occupants of the car as they move across the border. The action reaches its end with the explosion of the bomb. With Heston and Leigh's rush to the scene of the explosion a new action is begun.

Bazin also included as part of the so-called long-take style the characteristic of deep focus, which provides a view of the site of an action in which background as well as foreground are in focus. (Wide-angle lenses and other means were used by Welles in *Citizen Kane* to provide such a deep-focus perspective.)

The long-take, deep-focus style is valuable in that it tends to preserve the integrity of a situation's space (the deep focus) and time (the long take).

Bazin was referring to this integrity when he said of Robert Flaherty's *Nanook of the North* (1922):

> . . . It is inconceivable that the famous seal-hunt scene in *Nanook* should not show us hunter, hole, and seal all in the same shot. It is simply a question of respect for the

[7] Aristotle, *Poetics*, vii, 3.

Citizen Kane, *1940*

spatial unity of an event at the moment when to split it up would change it from something real into something imaginary.[8]

Thus, as Nanook the Eskimo hunter waits for the seal to appear in the hole in the ice, we see his whole act of waiting in expectation, poised above the hole with his spear ready. The long take assures this "respect" for the time of the event. At the same time, deep focus allows us to see the full environment in which the seal hunt takes place.

The long-take, deep-focus style also has the value of allowing for the discovery of motive and the appreciation of ambiguity in human action. As Bazin views human action, it has as an essential feature a certain quality of ambiguity or mystery. When, in everyday life, we perceive an action, we seek to ferret out the meaning of and intentions behind the action. We interpret gestures, looks, and reactions as indications of thoughts, feelings, and intentions, the meaning of some of which we have learned to discover over time. Films that involve us, move us, or aesthetically satisfy us engage this ability to seek out the meaning in human action for ourselves, while they leave room for some ambiguity as

---

[8] André Bazin, *What Is Cinema? Vol. I,* trans. Hugh Gray (Berkeley: University of California Press, 1967), p. 50.

well. Thus, Bazin's objection to montage style is that it so rigidly structures the audience's perception that it leaves little for it to discover and provides neither mystery nor ambiguity.

When in *Strike* (1926), Eisenstein cuts from the killing of an animal in a butcher shop to the slaughter of peasants by government troops, there is no ambiguity. The audience has no material for the imagination to use. That montage, whenever seen, will be the same. The montage in *October* (discussed above) that connects Kerensky with a peacock is another example of the rigid structuring of audience perception created by montage style.

The long-take, deep-focus style gives scope to our capacities for discovering motives and for appreciating ambiguity in action. With the continuous view of an action that the long take provides, we can seek out motive for ourselves rather than having our vision channeled as it is in Eisenstein's work. The deep focus makes us sensitive to the total environment in which action occurs, thereby enriching the material with which our minds must grapple in the search for the meaning behind action.[9] As we seek out motive and encounter ambiguity we become involved with the characters. This style gives talented actors scope for their capacities, too. Playing before the continuously running camera throughout one of the complete actions, an actress may draw upon all her resources for creating subtle, engaging patterns of behavior that will involve the audience.

The long-take, deep-focus style also has a potential for providing multiple perspectives on an action. When we see a film, we want to be able to adopt many viewpoints on the events portrayed. Some of the time we may want to identify with the protagonist, while at other times we may want to see things from a different viewpoint. Bazin's shooting style supposedly maximizes this possibility. With our vision unchanneled, and with the whole action and its environment spread before us, our propensity to shift to and appreciate different viewpoints is encouraged.

Because of the value he finds in the long-take style, Bazin is strongly inclined to claim that film can provide a vision of reality ordinarily denied to us:

> The aesthetic qualities of photography are to be sought in its power to lay bare the realities. It is not for me to separate off, in the complex fabric of the objective world, here a reflection on a damp sidewalk, there the gesture of a child. Only the impassive lens, stripping its object of all those ways of seeing it, those piled-up preconceptions, that spiritual dust and grime with which my eyes have covered it, is able to present it in all its virginal purity to my attention and consequently to my love.[10]

Stanley Cavell, a contemporary philosopher, has advocated a similar view. The core idea in his conception is that film enables its appreciators to perceive the world while viewing it, unseen, from what he calls "the condition of viewing as such":

[9] Ibid., *Vol. II*, pp. 61–82, 93–101. Bazin especially praises the films of the Italian New Realists (De Sica, Rossellini, Visconti) for their use of the long-take, deep-focus style to engage our perceptual capacities and our inclinations to respond to the mystery in human action.

[10] Ibid., *Vol I*, p. 15.

To say that we wish to view the world itself is to say that we are wishing for the condition of viewing as such. . . . Viewing a movie makes this condition automatic, takes the responsibility for it out of our hands. Hence movies seem more natural than reality. Not because they are escapes into fantasy, but because they are reliefs from private fantasy and its responsibilities. . . .[11]

By "automatic," Cavell indicates elsewhere, he is referring to "the mechanical fact of photography, in particular the absence of the human hand in forming these objects and the absence of its creatures in their screening."[12]

The echoes in Cavell of the Bazin quote are evident. There *is* something "automatic" about the cinematic medium that permits moviegoers to perceive without straining through "piled-up preconceptions," and "spiritual dust and grime."

Bazin tempers his view in a way that Cavell does not. Although he argues for the closest possible approximation of film image to reality, he is aware of the many limitations inherent in film that hinder a filmmaker's attempt to reproduce reality, and so he qualifies the correspondence he considers vital to make film art. According to Bazin, to recognize these limitations on correspondence one need only examine the process of selection as practiced in film. Choices made by the art-filmmaker—choices concerning visual elements *and* sound— while they may diminish reality, also have the effect, he says, of strengthening art. Bazin cites the example of the Italian neorealists, who were compelled by the inadequacy of their equipment to record the sound and dialogue of their films *after* shooting. This process of *sound looping* resulted in a loss of realism in that the natural synchronization of action and sound was sacrificed. Art was enhanced by this practice, nevertheless, because relations between visual elements and sound could be manipulated.

Cutting also prevents a reproduction of the real. In our everyday perception of objects, persons, and events, there are no interruptions such as those produced by cutting. When we shift our gaze from one part of a given location to another, it must pass over the intervening space. With cutting, the camera jumps from a view of one part of a location to another, omitting everything between. Cutting interrupts the flow of events by, frequently, giving us only fragments of what, in life, we could have followed through all stages. According to Bazin, these dramatic ellipses cause us to lose our grasp of the entire event.

Another feature that diminishes reality in the motion picture is the *significant event*. Bazin speaks of a "wonderful sequence" in Vittorio De Sica's *Umberto D* (1952) that contains *no* significant events:

The camera confines itself to watching her (the maid) doing her little chores: moving around the kitchen still half asleep, drowning the ants that invaded the sink, grinding the coffee. The cinema here is conceived as the exact opposite of that "art of ellipsis"

---

[11] Stanley Cavell, *The World Viewed* (New York: Viking Press, 1971), p. 102.
[12] Ibid., p. 73.

to which we are much too ready to believe it devoted. Ellipsis is a narrative process; it is logical in nature and so it is abstract as well. . . .[13]

The insignificance of the maid's morning activities is more real for its lack of dramatic ellipsis.

Other "unreal-making" features of the motion picture are the black-and-white image and the flatness of the screen image—obviously so because we see in color and in three dimensions.

Bazin's assumption, then, is that if there were no looped sound, no cuts, no dramatic ellipses, no significant events, and if the image were not black and white and flat, the impression of reality would be maximized. Andy Warhol's films *Sleep* (1963) and *Empire* (1964) might come to mind as films that would tend most in this reality-making direction. *Sleep* is little more than one incredibly long shot of a man during his eight-hour night's sleep, and *Empire* shows stationary split-screen views of New York's Empire State Building during an even longer period. They contain a minimum of the "unreality" features that Bazin mentions. Nevertheless, Bazin would not consider these films art, since, in his view, cutting, ellipses, significant events, and other such features must be employed in the making of an artistic film. This is the "aesthetic paradox" that Bazin speaks of as lying at the heart of any realistic style in the art film: that a "faithful reproduction of reality is not art."[14] Bazin fears that if the art film approaches the real too closely it may "become" reality and thereby lose its character as art. It is perhaps for this reason that he believes that an art film should be asymptotic[15]—closely approaching but never corresponding to reality.

Arnheim's Divergence Style

Rudolf Arnheim argues that films cannot fully portray the real, but that, in any case, the creation of the artistic film depends on a divergence from reality. He is insistent, however, that the film not divorce itself entirely from reality. His view therefore amounts to a position between those of Eisenstein and Bazin. Art occurs at those points in film where it exploits certain divergences from a completely faithful portrayal of the real that are inherent in the film picture.

Motion pictures diverge from reality in a number of crucial respects. First, the space of a motion picture is relatively flat. It is neither absolutely two-dimensional nor absolutely three-dimensional, but something between. The arrangement of objects in screen space can create a sense of three-dimensionality, but this perspective is counterbalanced by distortions in the images themselves. Of two ends of a table, for example, that end near the camera looks

---

[13] Bazin, op. cit., *Vol. II,* p. 81.
[14] Ibid., p. 64.
[15] Ibid., pp. 76–82.

far wider than can be accounted for by normal perspective. Arnheim cites overlapping as another phenomenon that reduces the sense of three-dimensionality:

> If (on film) a man is holding up a newspaper so that one corner comes across his face, this corner seems almost to have been cut out of his face, so sharp are the edges.[16]

The distortions in size and shape as well as these marked effects of overlapping, Arnheim believes, can be used to indicate importance, dominance, and significance.[17]

A second way in which film diverges from reality is through its lack of spatial-temporal continuity. Arnheim points out that:

> The period of time that is being photographed may be interrupted at any point. One scene may be immediately followed by another that takes place at a totally different time. And the continuity of space may be broken in the same manner. A moment ago I may have been standing a hundred yards away from a house. Suddenly I am close in front of it.[18]

A third divergence from reality deals with the black-and-white image, obviously different from the real world. The absence of color, however, focuses the attention of the audience on the compositions in the film picture—a great source of aesthetic experience.

While film does diverge from the real, Arnheim does not see its artistic potential as lying in a total divorce from reality. He does not agree with Eisenstein and other montage theorists that the art film should remold nature. An artist, he feels, should diverge from nature in certain respects, but not so far as to be unfaithful to nature:

> Any artistic medium tempts the artist to do violence to nature, and although it is fitting for the artist to submit to the conditions of his medium, it is on the other hand essential that he should not let himself be led into being unfaithful to nature.[19]

Of a montage depicting joy in Pudovkin's *Mother* (1926), Arnheim says:

> It is, moreover, very questionable whether the symbolic connection of smile, brook, sunbeams, "happy prisoner," and "joyous child" can add up to visual unity. It has been done thousands of times in poetry; but disconnected themes can easily be joined in language because the mental images attached to words are much vaguer, more abstract and will therefore more readily cohere. Putting actual pictures in juxtaposition, especially in an otherwise realistic film, often appears forced.[20]

The kind of creative remolding that the montage theorists advocate interferes with aesthetic structuring of the film. A montage sequence is contrived, while

[16] Rudolf Arnheim, *Film as Art* (Berkeley: University of California Press, 1957), pp. 12–13.
[17] Ibid., p. 63.
[18] Ibid., p. 21.
[19] Ibid., p. 137.
[20] Ibid., p. 90.

the same sequence shot with space-time integrity creates naturalness and unity.

Bazin's view that film becomes art when it closely approaches reality is also criticized by Arnheim, who welcomes film's divergence from reality and sees many artistic potentials in it:

> The creative power of the artist can only come into play where reality and the medium of representation do not coincide.[21]

Arnheim would no doubt cite Polanski's *Knife in the Water* (see Chapter 1) as an example of how artistic creativity comes into play when reality and film image do not coincide. Polanski's use of inconsistency of size to express the relationships between the boy and the couple is a prime example of divergence style. Had efforts been made to place the actors so that no inconsistencies of size were apparent to the viewer, the film's images would have been more in correspondence with the everyday look of things. They would not, however, have shown so vividly the changes that were taking place in the relationships between the characters.

The images in *Knife in the Water* are not marked by a divorce from the look of reality. Though an actor may look inordinately large in a setting because of placement close to the camera, the editing does not connect images from different times or places. Thus, the viewer has a vivid sense of the locale in which the action occurs. Certain distortions—like inconsistency of size—are present, but not in a way that interferes with what Arnheim would regard as a faithfulness to nature.

In Arnheim's theory, the film artist walks a tightrope. He must diverge from the real in order to create images with artistic quality, but he must not diverge too much.

Analysis of Eisenstein's Thesis

Eisenstein's theory emphasizes editing over photography. The simple shot can have an abundance of meaning; witness the opening long take in Welles' *Touch of Evil* (pages 43–46), which communicates much about characters, locale, and the dramatic situation. It also contains many interesting graphic and plastic patterns comparable in complexity to those of Eisenstein's montages.

Even in Eisenstein's *October* there are single shots of the leader, Kerensky, that exemplify his arrogance. When he postures in full uniform in front of his men, we see this aspect in his manner. The peacock montage is not necessary to our recognition of this, merely confirming what we have already recognized.

A shot is, indeed, a view of things that often comes charged with meaning and artistic quality. The Kuleshov experiment (page 85) carries no general implications for the nature of a shot. The fragments connected in the prisoner

---

[21] Ibid., pp. 109–10.

montages may not have meaning or artistic quality, but they are also not representative of the full range of material that can be captured in a shot. A view of a face often *does* require a context and interpretation in order for it to have meaning or aesthetic quality. It does not follow that other shots similarly require a context in order to have meaning or aesthetic quality. The opening long take in *Touch of Evil* shows characters from all manner of shooting angles and camera positions, providing rich material for evaluating the unedited content. It is not the case that all single shots are either too barren or simple to have meaning, graphic quality, plastic rhythms, or the like.

Eisenstein's arguments for the view that conflict is the essence of the art film are unconvincing. Though editing via conflict is brilliantly used in Eisenstein's own films, as we have seen, it is not necessarily the case that socially significant and aesthetically satisfying images must be structured in terms of this dialectical form. Among the film sequences discussed so far in this book, some were structured according to a conflict principle and some were not. There is no reason to believe that the nonconflict instances would have been better aesthetically or more powerful as vehicles for raising social consciousness had they been structured in terms of conflict.

Resnais' *Hiroshima Mon Amour* (pages 54–55), for instance, is structured in such a way that its powerful opening images are replaced in our consciousness by others. The theme of the film, meanwhile, is enunciated by the man Hiroshima. He reminds the woman, Nevers, that she will forget the important things that she should not forget. The film's affect thereby is unified with the theme of forgetfulness. The idea that the film seeks to communicate to the audience by dialogue and affect is socially significant: What happened at Hiroshima should not be forgotten, but it is a human propensity to do so. The way in which the film brings home to us the reality of the phenomenon of forgetfulness has its source in the *flow* of images, not in their conflict.

Each successive set of images takes its place slowly but surely in our consciousness. The latter images do not conflict with the earlier; they melt one into the other in a subtle, flowing way. Thus *Hiroshima Mon Amour* counters Eisenstein's claims for conflict as a structuring device of the artistic and socially engaged film.

The meaning and aesthetic quality of *The Last Picture Show* (page 23) also cannot be traced to editing by means of a principle of conflict. Its depiction of small-town American life of the early 1950s is accomplished in a unified way by similarity- rather than conflict-editing and by the look and movement of things within single shots. What the film shows about the time and place portrayed is that "everything is flat and empty here" (as is said at one point). Neutral camera angles, stationary camera positions, and medium shots predominate throughout the film. Their use conveys the humdrum, routine, and ordinary character of life in the town.

The *mise en scène* also creates a flat look. The sky is either completely clear or entirely filled with clouds. The effect is to diminish the viewer's sense of depth in the surroundings of the town. One thinks, by contrast, of a stock shot

in the typical western movie, where patches of clouds in the blue expanse
above give depth to the setting.

Editing in *The Last Picture Show* takes on an overall cyclical structure,
which conveys an absence of change or progress, providing us with a sense of
going back to where we started. A dust storm in winter begins and ends the
film. In the beginning, it seems Sonny's truck will hit the boy Billy; at the end,
Billy is killed by a truck. Sonny returns to the town, after his attempt to escape,
to Ruth, the middle-aged woman with whom he has had an affair, and to the
same kitchen table where it all started at the beginning of the film.

The unity and meaning of *The Last Picture Show* therefore does not come
about in a way that confirms Eisenstein's emphasis on editing in general and
editing via conflict in particular. Similarity, not conflict, is the principle at work
in making transitions. In addition, the vision of time and place that the film
provides depends in large part on what is captured by the photography within a
single shot.

The Last Picture Show, *1971*

The Cabinet of Dr. Caligari (Robert Wiene, 1920) is a landmark film that provides an important vision of the German society in which it was created. Its expressionistic settings, bizarre make-up and costumes, and stylized acting communicate this vision. The settings have the charm of Daumier, the intensity of Munch and Kollvitz, and the foreboding quality of Kafka. Most important, the viewer perceives these artistic qualities and the vision of authoritarianism in many cases in the substance of individual shots, not in conflict-editing.[22]

A filmmaker and theorist and a contemporary of Eisenstein's, Vsevolod Pudovkin, was also involved in the development of montage style. He, too, regarded art and meaning as characteristics that arose in the connection of shots rather than in what could be captured by photography in the single shot. In a Pudovkin montage, however, the root principle for editing was association, not conflict. In his "building-block" theory of montage, each additional image builds upon the previous elements. In a well-structured shot series (based on association) new meanings come into being that are not to be discovered in the individual shots that compose the series. A synthesis results from associating individual shots. As with Eisenstein, these elements may have no physical connection with one another. They may be drawn from different times or places.

In his film *Mother,* Pudovkin creates montages that fully rival those of Eisenstein aesthetically and in terms of significant social communication. *Mother* recounts the disillusionment and final martyrdom of a Russian woman in the prerevolutionary era. Her husband is killed in a strike. She betrays her son, Pavel, disclosing to authorities his actions on behalf of the workers. At Pavel's trial, she realizes the corruption in the prevailing system of justice, a realization that turns her into a rebel. She devises an elaborate prison-escape plan, which leads to the freeing of Pavel. In the ensuing action, however, both she and Pavel are killed.

In the sequence in which Pavel receives the news that he will be freed, Pudovkin creates a *plastic synthesis* in order to express the joy Pavel feels. Pudovkin felt that a single shot showing Pavel's reaction to the joyous news would be ineffectual.[23] Instead, a complex montage is created that combines widely disparate elements. From a close-up of Pavel's smiling face, Pudovkin cuts to shots of a brook swollen with spring water, of Pavel's mother as she walks away from the prison and the play of sunlight on the water, to a laughing child, and back to Pavel in his cell, jumping in an excited, joyous manner. Though not all of these elements are connected in space and time, they have associative connections with the upsurge of feeling that Pavel has at the news of his imminent release.

Next, Pudovkin shows how other prisoners respond to the news of the escape plan. A montage shows the men as they think of home in images of plows, soil, horses, and work in the fields. The prison-escape scene that then

---

[22] This observation is in no way inconsistent with the fact that there are some instances of conflict-editing in the film.
[23] Leyda, op. cit., p. 211.

follows gains power and momentum from its associative structure. With the addition of each "building-block" (each increment of marching workers, gathering people, and escaping prisoners) the whole increases immensely. The sequence builds tension and drama.

During the escape scene, the soldiers' movements against the rebels are broken into fragments on the screen. The rhythm of the cutting via association gives the action a crescendo-like character to which the excitement of the scene may be traced.

The shots of the workers marching in protest have a progression to them as well. As they march, others join them, increasing the size of the group. There is a growth in resoluteness as well, conveyed by a more rapid rhythm in the workers' march. Intercut with these shots of the gathering of marchers are shots of great masses of ice in a river. These ice masses flow in patterns, the size and direction of which parallel the patterned movements of the marchers. The ice masses are again seen at the end of the film, after the soldiers shoot Pavel and the Cossacks crush his mother. Their continual flow and seeming relentlessness symbolize the force and inevitability of the revolution.

The montages in Pudovkin's *Mother* that are built upon association do not seem to have less meaning or aesthetic quality than montages built upon conflict. Thus, even if editing were emphasized over what can be captured in a single shot, there are no compelling reasons for giving primacy to one style of editing (conflict) over the other (associative).

Analysis of Bazin's Thesis

Though Bazin is correct in pointing out the presence of meaning within single shots, his arguments advocating the closest possible correspondence between the film image and reality is deficient in certain crucial respects. While he points out many of the expressive potentials of visual elements and sound, he restricts too severely the cinematic means for their achievement. The long-take, deep-focus style that he advocates is only one of many ways to utilize visual elements and sound artistically. Furthermore, this style is not necessarily the best vehicle for realistic expression.

In Godard's *Alphaville* (page 7), a long take tracks the film's main character as he enters a hotel and proceeds to his room. Pillars, posts, mirrors, and darkness interrupt the audience's view of Lemmie Caution as he makes his way through the hotel. These objects, as they come between the viewer and the protagonist, create the effect of cuts in the long take. Thus the fact that a scene is portrayed by a single operation of the camera carries no implications for its realism. In fact, the important values that Bazin cites as resulting from the long take (space-time integrity, ambiguity, and the chance to view the action from many perspectives) are lacking in this long take.

The opening sequences from Kurosawa's *Sanjuro* (pages 13–14) also illustrate Bazin's overemphasis on the long take. These sequences are filled with abrupt cuts from one side of the action to the side directly opposite. Again, these reverse shooting angles fulfill Bazin's requirements of space-time integrity, ambiguity, and multiperspective. The views that they provide of the superhero samurai (Toshiro Mifune) and the nine inept young men he leads (the Nine) embody these qualities. Yet, we see not only Mifune's actions but also the reactions on the faces of the Nine—reactions that a long take, in place of these reverse angles, would not have captured.

Our capacities to discover the feelings and motives in ambiguous behavior is increased, not diminished, by these reverse shots. Moreover, the reverse angles do not have the effect that Bazin objected to in the Russian montage; the viewer's attention here is not fixed on a certain connection among objects to the exclusion of all else. Kurosawa's use of reverse angles provides multiple perspectives on the situation, leaving room for the viewer to find different qualities of the portrayed reality.

It is obviously true, as Bazin points out, that in our ordinary view of things there are no frames around space, no cuts from one part of space to another, no cuts revealing only part of an action, and no restriction to a single viewing angle. He sees these features as contrary to reality when used in film because they do not correspond to our everyday view. But when audience affect is considered, Bazin's view in this regard does not prevail. In Eisenstein's *October,* framing, cutting, and shooting angle combine to convey to the viewer Kerensky's state of mind. These features increase reality by heightening the audience's sense of the reality of the man.

Eisenstein starts with a relatively long shot of Kerensky alone in Czar Nicholas' library contemplating a decision to restore the death penalty. A cut is made to a shot in which the shooting angle remains the same but the camera is closer to its subject. Kerensky is now seen in a medium shot. The effect of the altered camera position is an increase in the size of Kerensky's image relative to screen space. A cut follows and we see an even larger Kerensky, who now dominates the screen. He signs the document restoring the death penalty, and a cut is made to a shot that diminishes his size.

Bazin would have advocated a long deep-focus take that would have maintained an integrated space and time. He would have wanted the whole of Kerensky's action to be shown without a cut. With such a long take, Kerensky's appearance and behavior would have corresponded more to the appearance of people in ordinary life settings. The viewers would be invited to draw upon their capacity to recognize Kerensky's feeling at this moment of decision—a capacity developed by their experience with real-life situations in which they have observed someone making a decision.

The *October* sequence reveals Kerensky's inner state in a way that requires the active participation of the viewer. Eisenstein uses a rather obtrusive cutting style as well as fixed framing and fixed camera position. These elements in the sequence allow the viewer to become sensitive to the sinister quality of Kerensky's action and to his inner effort in making the decision. His looming appearance, created by the changes in his scale relative to screen space, prompts the audience to interpret his action as sinister. The fact that he becomes larger relative to screen space bears no relation whatsoever to the way a man looks in a real-life space as he summons the courage to make an important decision. What the increase in image size does communicate, however, is his inner state of becoming big enough for the task.

Once the decision has been made, Kerensky's image shrinks. This shrinking expresses his return to a frame of mind in which he does not have to summon his inner resources. Thus, the framing, cutting, and camera position in *October* add realism to the sequence.

Apart from those aspects of it that deal with the portrayal of reality, Bazin's theory does not hold up with respect to the relation of film to the real in general. His recommendation that cinematic art be asymptotic in reproducing reality is misleading because there is no "danger" in a film approaching close to reality: No matter how realistic, there is no possibility that it will *become* the reality portrayed; at most, film can only *represent* it.

Bazin provides important concepts for understanding the expressive potentials of visual elements. The ambiguity of human action, the meaning contained within an integrated space and time, and the opportunity for viewing actions from many perspectives are all ideas that artistic cinema should explore. The long-take, deep-focus style, however, is not necessarily the best means to achieve them. Cinema's portrayal of the real can be extended beyond the Bazinian vista when affective powers of the medium are taken into consideration. Furthermore, the proposal made by Bazin, and extensively argued for by Cavell, that film provides a special vision of reality, reflects bias on the part of each toward photography over editing.

Cavell contends that the fact that "the projected world [the image on the screen] does not exist (now) is its only difference from reality," and that "ontologically . . . we see things that are not present."[24] In a similar vein, Bazin envisions a photograph as a visual mold. Yet the events of *Breathless,* for example, exist only within that film, brought into being by joining fragments of acting, poses, objects, lighting, and decor separately procured to enable the editing process to take place. The audience sees only the characters and the actions produced by this process. It is the *characters only* that exist now, in the film's time; they had no existence before the editing. Thus, to hold that *Breathless,* by virtue of being a film, provides us with a view of reality ordinarily denied us, is to give its images a status they do not have. The Bazin-Cavell view is grounded in an overemphasis on the photographic basis of the medium. Some films may get us to perceive things without our preconceptions intervening, but there is nothing intrinsic to the cinematic medium that makes this result inevitable.

Although Bazin and Cavell help us to appreciate the aesthetic potentials inherent in the single shot, we need to look beyond to a more balanced view, one that gives equal emphasis to photography, editing, and affect.

[24] Cavell, op. cit., pp. 24, 18, respectively.

Analysis of Arnheim's Thesis

Although Arnheim's divergence theory might seem an attractive middle position between montage and long-take theories, it is evident from his discussion of the relationship of film to reality that he has a restricted notion of the "real." When discussing reality he considers only the outward appearance of things.[25] Arnheim's analysis is sound so far as it goes: film does diverge from the real in appearance and many of its artistic potentials have their locus where there is this divergence. The concept of the real as it applies to film should, however, include inward stages—emotions and feelings. In this broader meaning, Arnheim's dual contention that film does and should, for artistic effect, diverge from the real is seen to be incorrect because his discussion omits the affective capacities of the cinematic medium. When *they* come into play in a motion picture, emotions and feelings can be faithfully and aesthetically portrayed.

Lenses used in filming, for instance, often create a divergence between film image and the everyday appearance of things. The loss of one dimension of realistic depiction, that of correspondence between film image and reality, can be offset, however, by exploitation of this divergence to help portray inward states.

Telephoto lenses give an image that seems "compressed" in depth, thereby distorting movement and the shape of objects and space. But they also can help portray human feelings, emotions, and thoughts—matters just as real as external appearance—via these compressions, distortions, and alterations.

A sense of what feelings can be represented by the use of telephoto lenses is provided by the following examples. In a crucial scene in Jean Renoir's *Boudu Saved from Drowning* (pages 49–50), Boudu wanders through the streets of Paris after he has lost his only companion, a dog. A telephoto shot of him roaming the banks of the Seine gives a sense of his alienation by creating the impression that a whole plane of objects (cars, buses, people) passes like a curtain between the audience and Boudu. He seems cut off from the viewer, and the audience from him. Nothing else in the film creates this awareness of Boudu's feeling of alienation and, when he attempts suicide, one thinks back to that telephoto shot for an understanding of his act.

Luchino Visconti's adaptation of the Thomas Mann novella *Death in Venice* (1971) contains a series of telephoto shots that are expressive of the state of mind of its main character, Gustav Aschenbach. Aschenbach, in Venice for a rest, goes, on his first night there, to the main hall of his hotel. Much of the scene is shot with a telephoto lens and conveys a sense of alienation much as in *Boudu:* A plane of objects seems to pass between camera position (Aschenbach's viewpoint) and the various sights within the hall. Sound editing supports the audience's impression of alienation from the action, as the dialogue fuses into little more than a dull roar. The viewer feels outside the action—a feeling matching Aschenbach's alienation as he sits alone. As in the case of

---

[25] Eisenstein, Bazin, and other film theorists share this problem with Arnheim.

Boudu, nothing else really gives the audience knowledge of Aschenbach's inner state; his face, his manner—none of these very clearly indicate his feeling of alienation.

Aschenbach sees Tadzio, a boy who is visiting the hotel with his family and who becomes a fatal attraction for him. As Tadzio joins his family in the hall, the viewer is not sure what the spatial relationship between Aschenbach and the boy is, since the viewpoint throughout is assumed to be that of Aschenbach. A sudden cut to a point behind Aschenbach (with the camera pointed toward Tadzio) reveals how close to Tadzio he has been all along. The prior uncertainty about spatial relationships is now clarified. The cut serves to emphasize the discrepancy between Gustav's physical closeness to Tadzio and his psychic distance from him. The distortions created by the long lens have given us another view of Gustav's inner feelings, in this case, emotional or psychic distance from Tadzio. Later, as Aschenbach compulsively follows Tadzio through the streets of Venice, it seems that he is physically close to the boy. But a change in camera angle and lens reveals him to be farther away than the viewer thought. Thus, changes in Aschenbach's state of mind are revealed through seeming changes (conveyed by the distortions of the telephoto lens) in the physical distance between him and the youth. Here a tightly knit structure depicts the progressive changes in Aschenbach's state of mind and also unifies the film. The aesthetic principle of unity coincides with a representation of the real—the changes in Aschenbach's psychic attitude.

A shot in Kurosawa's *Sanjuro* uses distorted movement and compression, created by telephoto lenses, to communicate the state of mind of a group of men. Toshiro Mifune stands before huge gates at the stronghold of the enemy. The camera is placed low to emphasize the height of the gates. At the same time, the telephoto lens compresses the view of a group of men of the opposing force riding out of the stronghold on a sortie. The compression conveys part of their group identity, their sense of themselves as a unit.

The lens serves another function as well, as it distorts the movement of the men so that each successive group seems about to ride over and crush Mifune. This illusion leads the viewer to sense with what indifference they would destroy anyone who stood in the way of their objective.

Inner states like the ones portrayed in *Sanjuro's* telephoto shot do not look a certain way or have specific forms.[26] A high correspondence with some reality in their representation cannot apply here. It is not by any correspondence of forms that a moviegoer grasps the brutality or group identification of the men, but rather by virtue of the distortions produced by the telephoto lens. The representational properties of *Sanjuro* are, therefore, partly dispositional: The film has a capacity (a disposition) to affect audiences. Those accustomed to movies shot predominantly with "normal" lenses will expect the protagonist to be crushed by the horsemen. An examination of the film's visual and sound

---

[26] By contrast, Monroe Beardsley, in *Aesthetics: Problems in the Philosophy of Criticism* (New York: Harcourt Brace Jovanovich, 1958), p. 270, defines depiction in terms of the visual appearance of things.

properties would not reveal the part played by its representational properties; only by taking affect into account will the meaning be discovered.

Besides rejecting Arnheim's claim that divergence is the source of aesthetic quality in film, there seems to be no reason for accepting his complementary claim that film should not be "unfaithful to nature." The plastic synthesis in Pudovkin's *Mother,* with its associative connections between different elements, is not without unity. Film images may be more concrete than the mental images that attach to words in poetry but it does not necessarily follow that their connections are therefore tenuous. Many of Eisenstein's montages, like those of Pudovkin, are unified even though they involve vividly concrete images drawn from very different times and places.

Probably the best example of this is a long sequence near the end of *October,* where images of religious icons from all over the world are linked in a dazzling display of editing skill. Though they are connected by their role as icons and by their centrality in their respective cultures, there is a conflict between the way the various gods are conceptualized and the way they are symbolized. As always in Eisenstein's work, this conflict serves to unify the sequence. Of this montage he writes:

> A number of religious images, from a magnificent Baroque Christ to an Eskimo idol, were cut together. . . . While idea and image appear to accord completely in the first statue shown, the two elements move further from each other with each successive image. Maintaining the denotation of "God," the images increasingly disagree with our concept of God, inevitably leading to individual conclusions about the true nature of all deities.[27]

Presumably the montage will lead to a questioning of allegiance and worship of king and country as well, a connection explicitly made in the sequence.

The connections that Eisenstein makes between the people's relationship to king and country and to religious icons, and the connection of conflict he makes between the concept and symbolization of God are not outside of or unfaithful to nature. We make many connections between things in nature. That we ordinarily do not think of the connections Eisenstein makes as part of nature is not a sign of their unnaturalness as much as it is an indication of how our perception of the connections of things is limited and conditioned. Perhaps it takes an Eisenstein to connect widely disparate things such as those found in the religious icon sequence of *October.*

Conclusion

In summary, the discussion has established that:

1. A film can faithfully represent the real but does not do so merely by

---

[27] Eisenstein, op. cit., p. 62.

means of its visual and sound qualities. Film's affective powers are at work as well.

2. If visual elements and sound are taken alone, films that represent the real cannot also be art. If, however, the affective capacities of film are mobilized, art and portrayal of the real can coexist.

3. Though a motion picture can represent the real, there is no aesthetic reason why it must do so. While the montage sequences of Eisenstein constitute a radical divergence from the real, they often embody both meaning and aesthetic quality.

We have seen that film can represent reality. Later (Chapter 8) we will discuss the cinematic style of realism, which is related to but also different from a portrayal of the real. The theories considered here do not encompass all viewpoints about the nature of film reality, though our analysis has brought out their crucial features. In Chapters 9 and 10 another important theory of film, that of structuralism, will be discussed in connection with the subject of film criticism.

the world that film creates

Taking events, characters, and situations as real or unreal in a film is dependent not only on our beliefs and expectations about the world outside the film (external beliefs) but also on beliefs and expectations created by the film itself (internal beliefs).

Many things happen within a motion picture that we would not expect to happen in "real life." Characters do things that run counter to the cause-and-effect regularities of our everyday existence. Chance occurrences and coincidences that would ordinarily defy credulity become acceptable by virtue of the flow of events—the context—of a film.

Within the world of film, King Kong becomes a real creature stalking the streets of New York City, an astronaut in the year 2001 enters a new dimension of existence where he achieves an expanded consciousness, James Bond takes on impossible assignments only to accomplish them with ease, and Dorothy walks the yellow brick road to meet the Wizard of Oz.

Not everything is real within the world of the film. Sometimes the artistic motivations governing the creation of the world of a film will dictate that some of the characters or events be portrayed as unreal. The death figure who walks the medieval landscape in Bergman's *The Seventh Seal* is such an unreal character. The appearance and acts of the Marx Brothers are effective comically in part because of their unreal portrayal within the world of the film.

The internal world of a film is not to be thought of as somehow a world shut up within itself; that is, the film does not typically create its own conventions for portraying objects, events, and characters. The factors that govern the workings of the world of the film have their source in the capacities of visual and sound elements to communicate in terms of cinema's affect and an audience's experience.

Reality Within the World of the Film

When a character seems real within the world of a film, but not outside it, we can accept her acts given the character or the world that has been established in the film. On the other hand, when we judge a character as real within the world of a film, we need not mean that she would not be believable outside it. The character's believability is judged by her relationship to developments within the story, and her actions, therefore, need not be taken as unreal as judged by reality—only as *real* in terms of internally generated beliefs.

Three of Stanley Kubrick's better-known films will be used here to identify the *real* within the world of the film. In each case some aspect of the film (its spaces, while at the same time investing it with some unusual quality. It is a The role of the aspect *within* the world of the film, however, renders it real in that world.

A Clockwork Orange

In *A Clockwork Orange* (1971) Stanley Kubrick has the problem of convincing the audience that what they see in the film is the immediate future. His artistic solution is to give space the familiar look and feel of our everyday spaces, while at the same time investing it with some unusual quality. It is a convention of our movie experience that the future brings with it a world that looks different. At the same time, if the space looks too unlike our everyday living space, the viewer will take the realm of the film to be one of fantasy. Kubrick uses wide-angle lenses to supply both the unusual look and a convincing quality of futurity. Space is partially in focus but there is none of the deep focus of *Citizen Kane.* The result is that everything looks very real, though the enclosed space has a box-like look, with slanting walls, that confers a quality of the unusual on the film's environments. The viewer, then, takes the space as both real and strange, which contributes to the sense of the immediate future.

A Clockwork Orange, *1971*

The workings of the world of Kubrick's film draw upon (1) the artistic potentials inherent in wide-angle lenses, (2) the audience's propensity to regard as real scenes shot in focus with normal lenses (because such films are the most familiar), and (3) the convention that spaces looking like those of the present cannot contain future events. None of these points is based on a convention created by the film itself; rather, *A Clockwork Orange* draws upon existing conventions that govern many movies.[1]

Dr. Strangelove

Dr. Strangelove (1964) is a satirical treatment of the incredible dangers of life in the nuclear age. In it an extremist air force general has found a flaw in the chain of command that permits him, without authority, to order nuclear bombing of "The Russkys."

[1] The fact that *externally* established factors, such as conventions, determine how the world of the work creates *internal* beliefs in the audience should not cause confusion regarding the distinction between internal and external beliefs. Internal beliefs are still held because of what happens within the film itself, not because of what the viewer believes to be true in the extramovie world. The point made here is that the film does not typically create its own conventions; it draws upon already existing ones.

Slim Pickens plays a pilot who has an especially zealous dedication to duty. Though an attempt is made to recall all planes from their mad mission, Pickens continues on. When the bomb-delivery system jams, Pickens mounts the bomb like a western movie hero on his faithful steed. He slaps at the jammed bomb release with his western-style hat until it releases. Like John Wayne in full attack on the Indians, Pickens whoops and waves as he rides to his collision with a Russian missile site.

To take Pickens' ride on the nuclear bomb as something an actual pilot would do is to miss the scene's marvelous satiric quality. Pickens' ride, though unreal in comparison with the real, is real within the world of *Dr. Strangelove*. The character Pickens plays is established as one who would do something this mad. To bomb the site is his mission, and he remains steadfast in his determination to carry it out.

The satiric tone of the film also contributes to the filmic reality of Pickens' ride. Pickens is but one of a host of overdrawn characters, in the context of which Pickens' ride seems fitting though unexpected; it is one final touch of satire that the viewer accepts as right in the circumstances.

2001: A Space Odyssey

Kubrick's *2001: A Space Odyssey* (1968) has a puzzling final sequence that is real only within the world of that film. The sequence, however, so radically violates the cause-and-effect relations we know from our everyday existence that it cannot be taken as representing the real. The film deals with man's evolution from a primitive state to the advanced, technical rationality of the year 2001.

In the concluding scenes, an astronaut in search of the source of some mysterious monolithic objects passes through an extravagantly fantastic environment of light, pattern, and color, to find himself in a room in which he is also present as an older man. As the sequence develops, he ages rapidly until he lies on his deathbed, a very, very old man. At the foot of his bed stands one of the mysterious monoliths. He reaches toward it in a final gesture of acknowledgment of its power. As the slab aligns with sun and moon, the astronaut is reborn as a "child of the stars."

Given our external beliefs, we will not think that such an aging process could actually take place or that the birth of a star-child could occur. The events of the final scene are, however, identifiable as real within the world of the film.

In the final scene the room is furnished in a style embodying the classical elements of order, clarity, and control, reflecting the thought of the eighteenth-century movement called the Enlightenment, which held rationality to be the highest human capacity. The process of comprehending the universe was seen as a never-ending one in which each new generation adds to the existent body of knowledge. No new dimensions of existence remained to be discovered; the world could be clearly understood, ordered into a desired form, and controlled.

The young astronaut's aging, then, symbolizes the theme that a man who has been exposed to a new dimension of existence cannot live according to this classical conception of reality.

In the room, the astronaut finds himself with the luxuries of his former life—real food and a real bed rather than the paste meals and hard, slab beds of space capsule existence. While eating, he knocks over a wine glass and, as it shatters on the floor, he contemplates the brittleness of it and of the life he leads. The shot's intent is reinforced when the astronaut looks quickly from the shattered glass to the deathbed where he lies.

Both the nightmare and the dream of science fiction are to be found in this final scene: the nightmare—that once man goes into space he will no longer be able to live as he did; and the dream—that once man goes to the stars he will be reborn into a new dimension of existence, with an expanded consciousness that provides instantaneous understanding of the universe.

Earlier events and developments in *2001* prepare us for what is to occur in the final scene. For instance, the brilliant display of light and pattern just before the astronaut arrives in the room connects in a most important way with it, giving, as it does, a view of the genesis and development of the universe. We see (in reverse order) evolutionary changes—star collisions, volcanic and water phases, ice advances—all punctuated by a shot of an eye, symbol of consciousness. The dazzling display is a visual expression of the astronaut's transcendence of the finite and his entrance into a new dimension, where he grasps creation as a whole in a single vision.

The space travel sequence of *2001* depicts man's attitude toward the universe as one governed by the classic conception. Space vehicles and apparatus are modeled after terrestrial forms. Some look like giant vertebrae, others like spermatozoa. A search vehicle looks and sounds like a hornet. The pods

2001: A Space Odyssey, *1968*

used for repairs are insectlike, and the suits of the repairmen make them look like burrowing animals. The seats in the space station resemble whale bones, and the space station itself is a huge wheel.

The connection between space travel and humankind's natural environment is graphically portrayed in the transition from the "dawn of man" sequence to the space travel sequence. An ape-man, joyous at his discovery of the concept "tool," impulsively uses a bone as a weapon—he throws the bone into the air, where, in the transition to the space travel sequence, it becomes the 2001 spaceship.

The banality, alienation, and dullness of most of the space travel sequence connects well with the themes of the final scenes. Though technology has made possible the wondrous adventure of space flight, it also dehumanizes those who work with it.[2]

The anticlassical theme that becomes explicit in the final scene, then, is foreshadowed by events depicted in the light display, the space travel sequence, and the opening scenes of the "dawn of man" sequence. The film creates the kind of world (with the particular evolutionary structure operative in it) within which the final scene is real.

Unreality Within the World of the Film

To be unreal within the world of a film, a character, object, action, or event must be inconsistent with its nature already established within the film. A humorously absurd example of such an unreal act occurs in Hitchcock's *Strangers on a Train* (see page 56). While Guy is occupied with the tennis match, Bruno, on his way to plant the cigarette lighter as evidence, accidentally drops it down a storm drain. Try as he may he cannot reach the lighter through the grill that covers the opening. At this point, Hitchcock interrupts by cutting to Guy and the tennis match. With the next cut we see Bruno recover the lighter, his arm seeming to stretch beyond human capability in the act. In terms of the physical circumstances and our internal beliefs about his capabilities, Bruno's act must be taken as unreal within the world of the work. The humor of the situation *demands* that it be an unreal act, and the viewer responds to a kind of Hitchcockian necessity: If the need is urgent enough in the world of the Hitchcock film, a character will find a way—even if it is impossible within that world.

Marx Brothers' Comedies

The comic style of the Marx Brothers represents another example of aesthetic uses of the unreal. One need look no further than the Brothers' make-up

---

[2] You may remember this sequence as one in which the computer, Hal, has more human qualities and personality than the astronauts.

and costuming to discover unreality. Harpo's wig is clearly a wig; Groucho's moustache is obviously painted on; Chico's accent is blatantly contrived. These transparencies—of wig, moustache, and accent—are the source for much of the humor. The fact that we see through them contributes to the zany humor by shattering the illusion of the existence of characters; we are constantly reminded that the Brothers are actors *pretending* to be characters.

Apart from costume, make-up, and accent, the Brothers' actions are unreal within the world of the film. In *A Night in Casablanca* (1946) a New York policeman appears, without explanation, in Casablanca. He asks Harpo, who is slouching against a wall, "What are you doing? Holding up the building?" Harpo nods, and the viewer quite naturally takes this interchange to be just another conventional old wisecrack. The cop then drags Harpo away, and the building collapses. Both the unexplained appearance of the New York cop and the collapse of the building will work comically only if we take them as unreal within the world of the film. The appearance of the New York cop in the exotic environment of Casablanca is not supposed to make sense or be in the least believable. The collapsing building occurs simply to undercut an old wisecrack. It is a transparent device analogous to the transparency of the Brothers' make-up and costumes.

In another scene in *A Night in Casablanca* the Brothers hide in the room of some men who are packing a suitcase and trunk. The situation demands that the Brothers delay the departure of the men, and, to do so, they unpack one container while the men are busy packing another, thereby continuously and systematically undoing all the packing. As the men pack, Harpo makes his way out of a walk-in closet, overturns a packed bag, and then scurries back into hiding. When the men discover the now unpacked bag, they think that they have had a lapse of memory. As the elaborate charade develops, Harpo and Chico sneak in and out of nearly everything that they will fit into, emptying and reemptying bags. When it occurs to the men to look for some hidden person in the room, their searches are absurdly feeble. Harpo and Chico evade their discovering gaze in the most preposterously simple ways, and the situation seems to the audience to be one in which some of the actors pretend that they are unaware of the presence and actions of the other actors—the Marx Brothers. The marvelous silliness of this packing scene has its source in our inability to believe that it is real even within the world of the film.

The Seventh Seal

The death figure that walks a plague-stricken land in Bergman's *The Seventh Seal* (1956) is also treated as unreal within the world of the film. This status for the specter of death is established largely by his relationship to other characters.

There before us on the screen the death figure is like all other characters in the film, but he is also visible only to a visionary juggler (Joseph), and to all other characters only at the moment of their death.

The Seventh Seal, *1956. Courtesy Janus Films*

The knight, Antonius Block, though he sees Death in the opening scene, delays his death to the end of the film by engaging Death in a prolonged game of chess. Though the knight remains a living character within the world of the film, it is clear that his perception of Death is like that of the others who are to die.

The manner of Death's appearances also contributes to his status as unreal within the world of *The Seventh Seal*. Without warning he appears on the seashore, as a priest in a confessional box, walking at the side of a wagon, and taking an accused witch to the stake.

As a character invisible to those with normal vision yet appearing suddenly and unannounced, the death figure becomes symbolic of the omnipresence of death in the disease-ravaged land of this film.

Fountain of Youth

Orson Welles' *Fountain of Youth* (1958) builds its satirical content upon a foundation of unreality. The "fountain of youth" in this vignette is a vial that rests upon the mantel in the living room of a young, attractive couple; she a starlet, he a tennis champion. A doctor has convinced the pair that the vial contains a drug that can preserve youth forever—but only enough for one, so the couple must decide which of them will have it. Much tongue-in-cheek humor results from their struggles to appear unselfish while obtaining the contents of the vial.

Substitutes for cutting contribute to an unreal atmosphere suitable to the farce. A set may darken for a few seconds, then lighten to reveal different props. Swish pans move us from one time or place to another. Some scenes are a series of stills showing characters in a succession of postures or attitudes. In one scene, Orson Welles' voice as narrator substitutes for those of the characters; in another, the vial glows with a magical light. Background music simulates the slow and awful ticking of a clock, indicating the passage of time as the couple ponders what to do about the vial.

Actions and delivery can only be taken as satiric: Gestures are overplayed, mannerisms are exaggerated, and responses are overblown.

The audience can relate to all of these unreal qualities of cutting and acting only as elements in a farce. The quality of unreality within the film is consistent. It builds up a momentum that makes each scene funnier than the last.

Chance in the World of the Film

The way in which a film weaves chance into the texture of its narrative determines much of its overall character.

A chance occurrence, though possible, is one that the audience believes would not occur. In a crazy comedy a man falling from a building toward certain death is saved when a truck full of feathers passes directly below. It *could* happen, but who believes that it *would*.

In a western, the occupants of a stagecoach are outnumbered and under siege. The end is near, when suddenly (out of nowhere) the cavalry appears. In a musical, a Hollywood star pursued by overzealous fans climbs atop a street-car and then jumps into the first passing car—a convertible. By another coincidence the car is occupied by a girl who will save his movie career and with whom he will fall in love.

There are films that are unthinkable without their network of chance occur-rences and coincidences—Max Ophuls' *The Earrings of Madame de . . .* , Stanley Kubrick's *Dr. Strangelove,* Rossellini's *Paisan.* Some filmmakers—Alfred Hitchcock, Luis Buñuel, Claude Chabrol—have made coincidence a controlling element in their style. Coincidence has even been made a conven-tion in various genres—witness the obligatory chance occurrences in the western and the musical.

Aristotle's remarks on the use of chance in the well-formed story have earned deserved attention:

> A likely impossibility is always preferable to an unconvincing possibility.[3]

> The right thing . . . is, in the characters just as in the incidents of the play, to seek after the necessary or the probable. . . .[4]

> . . . Incidents [arousing pity and fear] have the very greatest effect on the mind when they occur unexpectedly and at the same time in consequence of one another. . . .[5]

Though these reflections on chance have stood the test of time, a close examination of films where chance is crucial reveals some limitations of the Aristotelian view.[6]

Stagecoach

John Ford's classic *Stagecoach* (1939) has often been criticized for its gratuitous use of chance.[7] The scene described above in which the cavalry comes to the rescue is from this work. Examination of the film reveals that it does not fit the Aristotelian dictum that chance must be given an appearance of design.

The world created in *Stagecoach* is built upon well-known stereotypes and myths. The comic sidekick, the prostitute with the heart of gold, the dandy card shark, southern womanhood at its finest, the drunkard physician-philosopher,

---

[3] Aristotle, *Poetics,* 1460[a] (line 27).
[4] Ibid., 1454[a] (line 33).
[5] Ibid., 1451[b] (line 33).
[6] Aristotle intended his theories about the well-formed story to apply to dramatic tragedy. Since they have interesting applications to film, they have been measured against film here.
[7] "Chance" refers to such things as coincidences, improbable occurrences, luck and misfortune, and serendipity (the phenomenon of making favorable discoveries accidentally).

and the superhero all live up to their archetypal status. The prostitute nurses her wounded insulter. The card shark sacrifices himself for the southern lady. The doctor overcomes a bout with the bottle to deliver a baby. The hero asks the prostitute to marry him (she accepts) and single-handedly disposes of three men in a gunfight. The film also uses mythical ideas regarding fate. When the doctor-philosopher talks of fate, he prepares us for the chance appearance of the cavalry at the end. (As philosopher he knows the essential things about the world.)

Throughout *Stagecoach* a sense is cultivated in the viewer of the stagecoach as an irresistible force. In one scene it enters the gates of a relay station after surviving an earlier Indian attack. The gates seem huge and dark (by virtue of the set, lighting, and camera angle). Directly behind the gates are two large rock formations. As the stagecoach passes between these obstacles, screen center, it seems to be pushing them aside.

In most scenes in which it appears, the stagecoach dominates screen center, where most of the action also takes place. Subliminally, the viewer comes to regard the stagecoach's screen center location as a sign of its importance and dominance. For it to be denied its goal at the end by the Indians would be contrary to the expectations built up about its dominance.

The appearance of the cavalry, then, has mythic significance (given the archetypal nature of the story, characters, and action), fateful significance (issuing from the doctor-philosoper's earlier remarks), and internal significance (on the basis of the audience psychology developed by the use of screen space). The cavalry's chance appearance is not prepared for or motivated by plot or character, but it is felt to be "right" by an audience accustomed to themes built on stereotypes and myths and prepared psychologically for the event.

The Cousins

Claude Chabrol's *The Cousins* (1958) creates a cinematic space that engenders in the audience a feeling of the appropriateness of crucial chance elements. Chance occurrences in this film are unmotivated within the story, but the audience is prepared to accept them by the film's use of screen space.

As noted in Chapter 1 (see page 8), Chabrol's use of wide-angle lenses gives an unreal appearance to the world of *The Cousins*. Because these lenses instill a feeling of unease about the film's environment, the audience is prepared for shocking occurrences. In a world where things do not look quite right and where spaces have lost their dependable character, the viewer feels that something is bound to go awry.

Toward the end of the film, a series of coincidences lead to the accidental shooting of the naive country cousin, Charles, by the sophisticated city cousin, Paul. Charles, distraught, points a revolver at the head of a sleeping Paul. There is one bullet in the six-round cylinder of the gun. "You have six to one odds, I have one in six odds," Charles says. He pulls the trigger; the gun does not fire. In the morning, as Charles is concealing the gun, Paul appears. As he has done throughout the film, Paul takes the gun and playfully "shoots" Charles. This time the gun has the bullet in its chamber. Charles yells, "Don't shoot!" as the gun fires and he is killed.

In retrospect the act seems gratuitous. But as it is experienced the shooting seems appropriate to the film's reality.

Los Olvidados

Buñuel's Los Olvidados (1950) centers around the criminal activities of a young gang leader, Jaibo, and his relationship with Pedro, a rather innocent boy whom he is corrupting.

As the film begins, Jaibo leads his gang as they brutalize a blind man and rob and harass a legless man.

Jaibo and Pedro meet coincidentally in the film. Jaibo is waiting outside the reformatory gate at the very moment that Pedro is sent outside on an errand. In the final scenes, Jaibo is sleeping in the very place (a loft) where Pedro intends to hide.

Though they seem unmotivated, these meetings are important to the story's development. Pedro is sent on an errand outside the reformatory because the warden wants to give him a chance to show that he is trustworthy. Jaibo's corruption of Pedro at this point in the story is vital. Similarly, the meeting of Pedro and Jaibo in the loft is crucial because it results in the death of Pedro— one of the film's main characters.

It is the cinematic space of Los Olvidados and not the story itself that engenders a feeling of fittingness about its chance occurrences. Characters in the film often appear suddenly from just outside screen space. This mode of entrance engenders a feeling of unease in the viewer about the world of the film. In this reality, people are close by and seemingly always present.[8]

Jaibo particularly is given to appearing suddenly, with great impact on the film's action. We see his outstretched foot stop the progress of the poor, legless wretch who was harassed by the gang. During a later scene, in which a girl, Meche, washes her legs, we see Jaibo, but Meche does not. His sudden appearance surprises her. Upon arrival at a hiding place, Jaibo sees a waif, Little Eyes, and we see him lying in wait to surprise the child. Jaibo again appears suddenly on the occasion when he steals the knife from the shop where Pedro works.

The encounters with the legless man, Meche, Little Eyes, and Pedro largely determine how we will react to subsequent sudden appearances by Jaibo. Our sense of his presence has been well prepared by the time the supposedly coincidental meetings occur.

---

[8] Joe Saunders, "Los Olvidados," Pan (USC Cinema Publications), Vol. 2, No. 2 (March 1973), pp. 6–8.

The offscreen presence of characters in the film is uniquely reinforced by a few events that occur *within* its space. During a dream of Pedro's, we see Jaibo under Pedro's bed, where we have just seen the boy Julian whom Jaibo has killed. This offscreen-space presence of Jaibo (in Pedro's dream) implies that Jaibo occupies part of Pedro's unconscious.

Buñuel's treatment of the blind man is an example of another way in which this reinforcement occurs. On many occasions we see events that menace the blind man, but in a very strange way he "sees" them too. When the gang attempt to kill the blind man, the latter makes it clear that he knew what Little he senses their presence. When Little Eyes does not completely carry out an attempt to kill the blind man, the latter makes it clear that he knew what Little Eyes had intended.

When we next encounter the blind man, he is present at a street fight between Jaibo and Pedro. During the scuffle, he makes his way to the center of the action shouting, "Bandits. Bandits," for he knows that this is not simply a fight but a struggle for money and a knife. Later he tells the police where to find Jaibo, for he alone of the residents in the area knows where Jaibo is hiding.

The sense we as viewers have that people are present outside the screen space is varied in Buñuel's treatment of the blind man. Even though he is present in screen space, the blind man is characterized in such a way that he surprises us as much as other characters who suddenly appear from outside of screen space. The uneasiness we feel regarding the blind man is not caused by our sense of his evil (as with Jaibo), but by a sense that, because he is blind (and therefore helpless), he will ultimately be killed.

The accumulation of these experiences of offscreen presence (and variations of them) determines the viewer's reaction to Jaibo's "coincidental" presence outside the reformatory and in the loft. Though they are unmotivated in the narrative, one feels that he was bound to be there.

The Thirty-Nine Steps

Alfred Hitchcock uses chance in a variety of ways. Most frequently he assaults us with an unbelievable series of chance events, causing us to suspend our disbelief. So many chance events occur that the the viewer begins to anticipate (with a readiness to accept) the next ridiculous coincidence or gross improbability.

In Hitchcock's 1935 classic *The Thirty-Nine Steps* Robert Donat is rescued from danger by a series of events that cannot be believed either through reliance on what we know of the extramovie world or by what happens within the film itself.

Donat, implicated in the murder of a woman at his flat, leaves London to escape false charges about to be be brought against him. His flight takes him to a place in Scotland where the murdered woman told him a spy ring had its headquarters. On the road he happens on a farm. The couple who live there invite him in. When police appear, the farmer's wife gives Donat her husband's coat to disguise his getaway. Later, when the spy-ring leader shoots him, Donat's life is saved by the farmer's hymnbook in the breast pocket of his coat. Donat later tells the police the circumstances surrounding the woman's murder, but when they do not believe him, he is forced to flee again by jumping through a window. In the confusion that follows, Donat escapes by joining a Salvation Army band that is coincidentally passing by at just that moment. Donat ducks from the band into an alley that leads him straight to a conference hall where he is mistaken for the overdue speaker.

Donat improvises a speech while a woman and two men, who are part of the spy ring, enter. The men feign connection with the police, but once Donat has been hustled into their car, he discovers their identity. Chance again comes to the rescue, this time in the form of a heavy blanket of fog and a large group of sheep. The sheep block the road at just the right time to permit Donat's escape.

Though Hitchcock piles up these coincidences and improbabilities, he tempers the viewer's sense of incredulity somewhat in order to keep the film from lapsing into mere farce. Often he will hide them from the viewer's attention. In the sequence where the farmer's hymnal saves Donat's life, the interval between receiving the coat and the occasion of its saving his life is considerable, and it is not until a considerable time after he is shot that the hymnal's role is disclosed.

From the time Donat hurls himself out of the police station window, Hitchcock steadily increases the pace of the action, leaving the audience little opportunity to pause and consider the improbability of it all.

Still another Hitchcock hiding technique is distraction. While the spy-ring people make their implausible entrance into the conference hall, the viewer is distracted from their entry by Donat's fumbling attempts to improvise a speech.

Conclusion

Aristotle's principles for the portrayal of chance events are limited to only some of the elements of the work of art. In their application to film they are only valid for the visual/sound qualities of the movie. When a film utilizes the affective powers of the medium to give its viewers a sense of the appropriateness of chance events or to elicit a reaction that prepares them for coincidences, Aristotle's theory is not fully adequate.

A film can create its own reality. It does so by engendering in us what may be called internal beliefs, expectations, or reactions. Viewers interpret an event or action as real or unreal within the film because of the connections between visual elements and sound and sometimes also because of the reaction they have to what they see and hear.

The conventions that the filmmaker relies upon are not typically created by the film itself. They are rather functions of the audience's experience.

uncertainty
in
cinema

We have seen that a sorting out of events, actions, characters, and situations into what is to be taken as real or unreal is fundamental to our experience of motion pictures. In cinematic surrealism the viewer is intentionally left *unsure* whether the things or events in the film are to be regarded as real or unreal.

The *uncertainty* distinctive of cinematic surrealism is not *ambiguity*.[1] An ambiguous element is one that is difficult to interpret, but not with respect to its reality or unreality. It is the latter type of problem with which the surreal is involved.

The *uncertainty affect* will be traced through the various cinematic contexts in which it functions. These contexts, though employed by filmmakers using all types of styles, are typically associated with the work of surrealists. They include dreams, chance and coincidence, radical juxtapositions, transformations, displacements, and identity changes.

[1] The concept of surrealism developed here is phenomenological. It has to do with the way phenomena appear to an observer, quite apart from what may really be there.

Surrealist Dreams

Luis Buñuel has been one of the great practitioners of surrealism in film. His remarkable career extends from the silent era, when he made *Un Chien Andalou* (1929) in collaboration with surrealist painter Salvador Dali, to the present. He remains one of the world's leading directors. In Buñuel films, a frequent vehicle for the surreal is the dream or seeming dream.

Belle de Jour

Virtually all of *Belle de Jour* (1967) could be a dream, although the viewer is confronted with this possibility only in the final scene. Until then, *Belle de Jour* seems to be a straightforward narrative of events in the life of an upper-class married woman who lives her daytime life as a prostitute.

The opening sequence seems to portray events that are to be taken as real. As husband (Jean Sorel) and wife (Catherine Deneuve) ride in a carriage through the Bois de Boulogne, they talk quietly of their feelings for one another. Suddenly Sorel orders the carriage stopped. He has Deneuve tied to a tree and his drivers lash her with their riding whips. He then tells the footman, "She's yours now." When the footman touches her, she looks at him with repugnance and pleasure. Just as the footman kisses Deneuve's back, Sorel, off screen, says, "What are you thinking about?"

There is a cut to a medium close-up of Sorel, with his back to the camera, in their Paris apartment. She replies, "I was thinking of you . . . about us." The viewer realizes that this opening scene was Deneuve's daydream. Thus, from the very first scene, the viewer has the impression that the film may not actually be as it seems.

The story develops, with Deneuve drawn to a bordello where she becomes a prostitute under the name "Belle de Jour." A customer, in love with her, shoots her husband, leaving him paralyzed.

Near the end of the film, Sorel sits helpless in a wheelchair in the living room with Deneuve. A medium close-up shows a tear glistening on his cheek. Again (as in the opening sequence) Sorel asks Deneuve what she is thinking of. "I was thinking of you," she again replies. Suddenly Sorel gets up from the wheelchair, strides across the room, and fixes two drinks. The sounds of cowbells and horse hooves gradually infiltrate the scene as they talk, then give way to the sound of a carriage—the same carriage we heard and saw in the first scene.

It is impossible to know how much of the film records Deneuve's daydreams and how much is to be taken as reality. Are none, some, or all of Deneuve's visits to the bordello daydreams? Her husband was not paralyzed, as we were led to believe; or was he, and was she fantasizing that he could walk? The viewer is left uncertain.

Nazarin

In Buñuel's *Nazarin* (1958) a prostitute, Andara, lying in bed at night, has an extraordinary experience that produces the uncertainty affect in us. The camera moves in on her and then cuts to a portrait of Christ. The portrait, when seen earlier, was a standard portrayal; now it depicts a grinning, mocking Christ. A cut is made back to Andara and, as the camera moves straight back, away from her bed, a new (faster) rhythm is established. We hear a cry from off screen and see Andara covering her face. She looks toward the source of the cry, shrinking from the agony it seems to express. A cut is made out into bright sunshine to the source of the mournful cry: a child who has been spanked by its mother. In the next shot, Andara rises from her bed, which is now bathed in morning sunlight. A blind man passes the mother and the child she has just spanked and knocks on the door of the building in which Andara is staying. This movement establishes the physical relationship between the child's cry and the room where Andara heard it.

The scene's inconsistent lighting creates uncertainty. If the viewer takes Andara's response to the child's cry naturalistically, then she has responded at night to an event occurring during the day—an impossibility, requiring that this scene be regarded as unreal. If, on the other hand, the viewer regards the cry to which Andara responds as being *in* a dream she is having, then one has the impossible task of explaining the daylight shot of the crying child.

Tristana and *Wild Strawberries*

Dreams are used to create similar surreal effects in Buñuel's *Tristana* (1970) and Ingmar Bergman's *Wild Strawberries* (1957).

In the Buñuel film, the protagonist, Tristana, sees her guardian's head as the clapper in a church bell. From this scene, an abrupt cut is made to her waking in bed, leaving viewers feeling they have been viewing a dream of Tristana's. However, since there is no discernible beginning point for the dream, the viewer wonders where it began. Furthermore, the scene does not develop in a dream-like way.

Just the reverse occurs in Bergman's *Wild Strawberries*—namely, what seems to be a dream has a beginning but no ending. The film's main character, an old professor, Isak Borg, is on his way to Lund, where he is to receive a prize for his distinguished work. His trip is marked by spatial dislocation. There is much reversing of camera direction in cuts that leave the viewer unable to visualize a coherent space.

Borg seems to have the daydream in a scene in which he stops at his childhood home. There are conventional indications of a cinematic daydream: The lighting takes on an overexposed look, treetops wave slowly, clouds float by overhead, and Isak's pose becomes reflective. While remaining an old man, he moves about among people and events of his childhood. He talks with a girl,

Sara, on whom he had had a crush as a youth, and it seems that these extraordinary events must be taken as part of a daydream.

This interpretation is undermined, however, when at the end of the sequence Borg walks out of the house, with no discernible transition, directly into the present. It appears that he has had a daydream with a beginning but no ending. Confidence in the daydream interpretation is undermined further: Walking out of the past directly into the present, the old man meets another Sara, a present-day Sara. Both Saras are played by the same actress, adding to the viewer's bewilderment about how to sort out the reality of Borg's walk into his past. The accumulation of reversals and inconsistent elements makes the viewer's perception of Isak's acts ever more doubtful; since there is no end to the dream, perhaps there was no dream after all.

The viewer of these dreams in the Buñuel and Bergman movies cannot believe that the guardian's head was in fact a bell clapper or that Isak Borg could walk physically into his past; neither can these sections simply be consigned to the category of dreams. Because the "dreams" have either no beginning or no end, viewers may think that they are to be taken as things that *could* have occurred. These contrary reactions balance out one another to leave the viewer uncertain of how to react.

Chance in Surreal Cinema

Chance is used in the surreal film to bring about a balancing of external and internal beliefs. Events that the audience, relying upon external beliefs, thinks would not happen do, in fact, happen in the film. As such, they fit the characterization of chance events discussed in the previous chapter. Unlike the cases discussed here, however, their occurrence in surreal film is not prepared for by developments within the world of the film, and it is impossible to identify them as either real or unreal within that world. As a result, when these chance events occur, the uncertainty affect is created.

The Exterminating Angel

One of Buñuel's most striking surrealist effects occurs in *The Exterminating Angel* (1962).

In it, guests at a dinner party retire to the host's salon, where they find themselves unable to leave. Days pass. Loved ones, public officials, bystanders, and others outside the house cannot enter. At one point, they realize that by chance they have all returned to the locations they had when they began their strange confinement. One guest suggests that if the woman who was playing the piano when they became imprisoned would play just as she had at that moment, they would be free. She plays, and the guests' belief in the powers of this device releases them from their confinement.

That the guests give themselves and each other reasons for remaining at the party is an important element in the film's surreal effect. In so doing, the audience's doubts as to how to view their entrapment are increased. For, given our beliefs about human motivation, we cannot regard the coincident inability of so many people to leave the party as real. We know that it cannot occur in the extra-movie world. Yet the reasons that each guest gives for staying in the salon are in and of themselves reasonable enough.

Our beliefs are challenged by the film. Because the characters' actions—apart from their confinement—can be taken as natural, the viewer is inclined toward the interpretation that in the world of *The Exterminating Angel* the confinement is real. But the characters' ridiculous belief that their imprisonment can be dispelled by a coincidental return to their previous locations in the room seems so unreal that the viewer is left not knowing what to think.

Rosemary's Baby

Roman Polanski's adaptation of Ira Levin's book *Rosemary's Baby* (1968) seems laced with coincidence after coincidence. But if one takes the film as a realistic depiction of witchcraft, there are no coincidences. Just which standpoint the viewer is supposed to adopt is impossible to determine.

Rosemary and her husband Guy move into a new apartment. She is pregnant, and the couple next door recommends an obstetrician. Because he wears a tannis root charm, which, she has read, is associated with witchcraft, Rosemary becomes suspicious. In a nightmare, which follows, Rosemary's husband changes into the devil and rapes her while the next-door neighbors look on. In the midst of the nightmare she screams, "This is not a dream; this is reality." The next morning she finds marks on her body that her husband admits to having made while she slept.

Eventually Rosemary feels so threatened that she flees. As she desperately tries to phone a doctor whom she trusts, a man who looks like the feared doctor appears.

The audience has to decide how to view these "chance" events: Is Rosemary deluded and are these events merely coincidences? Are there people next door who bring about all these happenings, but who have no supernatural power? Do the next-door neighbors and Guy really practice witchcraft?

The film is structured so that none of these alternatives take precedence in the viewer's experience of the film. One is left in the state of uncertainty characteristically produced by surreal films.

Juxtapositions and Transformations in the Surreal

A device favored by surrealists is the use of bizarre and sometimes shocking juxtapositions. This is usually accomplished by putting something where it does not seem to belong, thus rendering the reality of things and events problematic.

Buñuel's films contain many examples of use of this device. In *The Exterminating Angel,* a tuxedo-clad young man shaves his bare legs with a razor, and chicken claws fall from a woman's handbag in the middle of the host's elegant salon; in *Los Olvidados* (1950), donkeys, chickens, or doves are inexplicably present whenever major events occur; in *Viridiana* (1961), there is an incredible feast of the beggars in which an orgy of the deformed takes place to the sublime strains of Handel's *Messiah.*

Un Chien Andalou

Buñuel's *Un Chien Andalou* uses juxtapositions and transformations (in which one thing becomes another) extensively to create its surreal quality. Most shocking and famous of these is one in which Buñuel himself acted. In the scene he stands before a window sharpening his razor. A cloud passes across the moon. He then slices open a woman's eye with his razor blade. The mood is transformed from tranquility to horror. The similar visual patterns—a thin object passing through a round one—have been juxtaposed as if they could be considered equivalent. The connection between the two images is so

Un Chien Andalou, *1929*

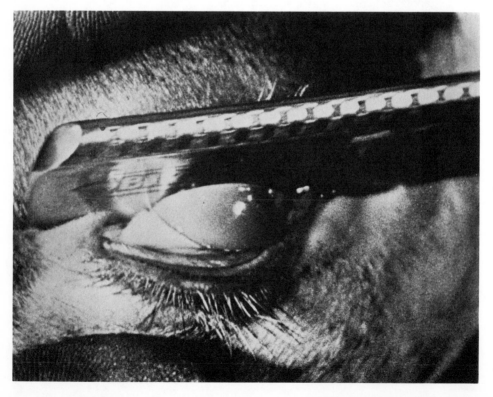

abstract that the viewer finds it difficult to identify the tone of the film. Is it just a series of images with a poetic connection, or are the events of the film to be taken in some other way?

The remainder of the seventeen-minute film offers similar situations. A naturalistic texture is established, followed by something that seems out of place and involves a transformation. One character seems normal enough until insects suddenly crawl from a hole in his hand. To make the situation even more difficult to identify with respect to film reality, the hand is shown in close-up, and we see that it is merely a prop.

In another scene, a man is making aggressive advances toward a woman. She retreats across the room, seizes a tennis racket, and holds it like a weapon. The man, seemingly searching for something, picks up two ends of rope from the floor and starts pulling with great effort some object that is off screen. The woman, looking off screen, expresses shock at what he is pulling. Finally we see what it is: two grand pianos with the decaying carcasses of two donkeys draped over them. Two priests lie below, praying and allowing themselves to be pulled along in this horrifying procession. Their mood changes abruptly from unconcern to shock.

The change that it brings to the tone of the film and the bizarre juxtapositions that it embodies leave us bewildered.

Time in *Un Chien Andalou* is also strange and incomprehensible, there being no chronological development. From the first scene, we shift forward to "eight years later," then backward to "sixteen years before." The final scene takes place "in the spring."

On one occasion, the door to an apartment opens on the ocean, but the apartment has been seen to be high above a street. Are the events of the film to be taken as in some way realistic? Are they in someone's dream? Are they to be taken as purely abstract? We do not know.

Land Without Bread

Buñuel's *Land Without Bread* (1932) is a surreal documentary, contradictory as that may seem. It documents a group of people called the Hurdanos, who live in a remote area of Spain in the most wretched poverty. The film's method of juxtapositions and transformations is manifest primarily in the relationship between the visual elements and the narration.

The narrator is representative of civilized Western culture. His assessments of the "primitive" culture of the Hurdanos reflect his cultural bias. Condescendingly, he tells us how Hurdano customs and artifacts resemble those of his own background. He notes how the cut paper and the pot covers show a flair for interior design. He describes ornaments worn by a child at a ceremony as strange and barbaric. At the end of the film, the narrator indicates that he left the Hurdanos, not to return—an act that sums up his involvement with their situation.

The background music has a similar relationship to the Hurdanos. The strains of Brahms' *Fourth Symphony* accompany the sights of misery. Taken in conjunction with the narrator's attitude, it most vividly reflects an élite culture that cares nothing for the plight of unfortunates. Over and above what it represents in juxtaposition to the tribe, the background music is incongruous in that its climaxes have no correspondence with the scenes and actions shown. The music will build and build to a great climax, while the visual elements build to nothing. Some of the asynchronousness of music with visual elements is so marked that the scenes become humorous. The film is so bizarre that we feel it might be appropriate to laugh, even in light of the misery being shown.

In many scenes, the narrator describes and the camera shows the horrifying circumstances in which the Hurdanos live. In other scenes, the narrator simply recites facts about the area ("Fifty-two towns with a population of eight thousand." "We can classify two hundred species of trees."). His lack of expression in describing these very different things is unsettling. The viewer expects some alteration in expression, but gets none. At one point the narrator tells of a girl in a Hurdano town who sickens and dies. His totally dispassionate tone strikes the viewer as incongruous given the subject.

Buñuel manipulates the environment to make it seem even more grotesque than it is. Hurdano idiots are supposedly shown in their environment, but we feel that the whole event is staged for the camera. A goat is shot and sent hurtling down a cliff to "illustrate" how goats sometimes slip to their death off the cliffs. The camera work is amateurish, yet Buñuel is a skillful filmmaker, so one must consider that the bad photography is intentional.

Transformations become an important feature of the film via Buñuel's so-called "yes, but" structure, which many commentators have mentioned.[2] In it the narrator and camera reveal something terrible concerning the Hurdanos. Then some hope is offered. When we are lulled into the expectation of some improvement or salvation, the situation is changed and we find that it is worse than we had thought. For example, we are told that the Hurdanos are bitten by vipers, but that the bites are not fatal. We then are informed that the medicines used to counteract the venom sometimes are. The narrator tells the audience that villagers nearly starve during the winter, but that when spring comes they have wild cherries to eat. It is then revealed that the fruit gives the people dysentery.

The accumulation of horrifying and inexplicable juxtapositions of visual elements and narration, the attitude of the filmmaker, and the transformations supplied by the "yes, but" structure eventually render the viewer incapable of feeling regarding the events of the film. Are things really like that in Hurdano country, when some events are clearly staged for the camera's benefit? What is to be made of the incongruities? Why is the film so repetitious? If the film is supposed to expose the indifference of our culture to the suffering of others,

---

[2] Adonis Kyrou, *Le Surréalisme au Cinéma* (Paris: Terrain Vague, 1964).

shouldn't it make us feel, not desensitize us? The film's surrealism has its locus in these problematic questions.

Los Olvidados

Startling juxtapositions are exemplified in *Los Olvidados* when the gang assaults the blind man. The scene is punctuated with a hen cackling at the victim nose-to-nose as he lies on the ground. It is noteworthy that a particular musical instrument substitutes for the sound of the hen here and in crisis situations throughout the film. It is used when Pedro's mother beats her fighting rooster and hens; when Pedro throws an egg at the camera, fights with some boys, and beats a chicken to death; and when Jaibo kills Pedro in the loft. In this last scene, a chicken steps on the dead Pedro's face.

Such musical substitution has the affect of removing the actions of the chickens from the naturalistic texture of *Olvidados.* We are not sure whether to view these actions as real or unreal. Although this affect probably works on a subliminal level, its importance is not to be underestimated, especially since the film is otherwise so vividly concrete.

In addition to this nonnaturalistic use of sound, a system of associations is established in connection with the chickens that plays a central role in the creation of the uncertainty affect. The viewer does not know if the chickens (and animals in general) have a causal connection with some of the events of *Olvidados.* There are many images that indicate animal involvement: The blind man rubs a dove across the back of a woman to cure her back trouble; in the loft, cackling chickens alert Jaibo to Pedro's presence, thus playing a role in his death at Jaibo's hands; a donkey looks in at the window of Meche's house, seeming to summon her to where Pedro lies dead; a pariah dog passes slowly and eerily along a bar of light that falls across the dying Jaibo.

The animals are there in juxtaposition with the film's crucial events; the audience has somehow to relate them.

Entr'acte

René Clair's *Entr'acte* (1924), like *Un Chien Andalou,* is built entirely on startling juxtapositions and transformations. The film has been described as an exercise in pure movement.

In its opening scenes one sees men famous at the time in the arts in France (including artists Man Ray and Marcel Duchamp, and composer Eric Satie) playing chess on a high building and hunting birds on a skyscraper. Their familiarity to the initial audience (as artists, not actors) added to the incongruity of the situation. For later audiences, the juxtapositions are radical enough without recognizing the famous personages.

In addition to the juxtaposition of men in hunting regalia with the top of a skyscraper, we see an ostrich egg suspended on a jet of water, a cannon seemingly propelling itself on screen and coming to rest pointing directly at us.

Startling changes then occur. The Paris square, Place de la Concorde, materializes on the chessboard; the ostrich egg remains suspended in midair after the water jet has been turned off; a dancing ballerina, her face at first obscured, is revealed to be made up to look like a bearded man; the egg becomes a target for the hunters, after which it becomes ten eggs on ten fountains.

The set piece of *Entr'acte* is a strikingly irreverent funeral scene. In it society—dressed in white—gathers for the funeral of one of the hunters, who has been accidentally killed. The camel-drawn hearse is decked with hams, paper chains, and publicity posters. The "mourners" eat the funeral wreaths hanging on the sides of the hearse. They throw rice as the hearse departs. It breaks away from the camel and begins to travel on its own with the mourners in hot pursuit. The chase alternates between fast and slow motion with some tracking shots. Shots of a roller coaster are intercut. The coffin falls from the hearse and the corpse miraculously rises from it. Dressed as a conjuror, the hunter, with much waving of a magic wand, makes everyone in the funeral procession-cum-chase disappear. The picture fades out, the word "End" appearing painted on a paper held up to the camera. The audience is led to believe that the film is over, but a final undercutting of our expectations occurs when a man jumps through the paper (bearing the word "End") in slow motion, and the film's characters follow him. Transformation thereby carries through even to the ending of the film.

Orpheus

Jean Cocteau's films are filled with startling juxtapositions and transformations. *Orpheus* (1959), his major achievement in film, derives from the ancient myth of Orpheus, who beguiles the ruler of the underworld (Hades) with his music in order to recover his dead wife Eurydice.

Cocteau's film portrays the love of a modern poet, Orphée (Jean Marais), both for Eurydice and for the Princess (Maria Casarès), a death figure whose frequent journeys into this world have endowed her with human emotions. Thus she can return Orphée's love and feel jealousy—the reason she has Eurydice killed. When Orphée goes into the underworld seeking Eurydice, he also searches for the Princess. Killed in a fight, Orphée is restored to life by the Princess and her chauffeur, Heurtebise.

As an ancient myth fully embedded in the world of the present, the film is one overall transformation. The Princess is hardly the horrifying specter of Bergman's *The Seventh Seal,* though she is every bit as otherworldly. Though dressed in symbolic black, her beauty masks the horror of death. Her presence in this world is forcefully expressed by her possessions and retinue. She drives a Rolls-Royce and is accompanied by executioners who, dressed as policemen, ride motorcycles and carry machine guns.

Transformation is a recurring thematic device as well. Characters pass through a magical mirror into "the Zone"—the other world, where the miraculous can happen. The boundaries between the two worlds are not clearly drawn. Characters die and are transformed (in the Zone) into the living.

Orphée goes to the other world without any discernible change, producing a melding of the two worlds that gives rise to the uncertainty affect. The passage from one world to the next cannot be taken in an easy way as a transformation—as a moving between the real and the unreal. We do not know what is supposed to be the real—both realms or, if one, which.

The bizarre juxtapositions created by presenting the agents of death in modern trappings brings about a similar kind of melding of the two realms. The natural response of the viewer is to regard the action in front of and behind the mirror as at one with respect to their reality, whatever that status may be.

Two Men and a Wardrobe

Roman Polanski's early film *Two Men and a Wardrobe* (1958) turns on a variety of ironic juxtaposings. Making the viewer constantly shift his viewpoint is the dynamic of the film. It opens with two men struggling out of the sea carrying a huge wardrobe with a mirror on one of its sides. This seeming mood of fantasy is at odds with the purposeful manner with which they walk about with their burden. It begins to seem plausible that the acts of these characters in the world of this film are to be taken as real. The two carry the wardrobe everywhere and other characters accept its presence: At one point, a man checks his appearance in its mirror.

This kind of naturalistic texture is, however, disrupted in subsequent scenes. It becomes evident that important things happen wherever the wardrobe passes. In one especially shocking juxtaposition, the men are carrying the wardrobe in a natural setting; close by a man is being beaten to death. In another, a character stealthily picks the pocket of another as the wardrobe passes. Displacement is at work in this scene as well: The music, which has ironically commented on the action throughout is taken up in this scene by the pickpocket, who whistles the theme of the background music.

In one scene we see what looks like a fish in the sky. The camera eventually reveals that we are seeing a reflection in the wardrobe's mirror. This juxtaposition of fish and sky and the transformation of unreal appearance to real reflection makes us pause to question the reality of the film.

At the end, when the audience has become thoroughly confused—as to whether the two men and their wardrobe are meant to be real, fantasy, wholly symbolic, or agents of the evil that follows their passing—the men walk quite naturally across a beach (where a child has established a highly ordered landscape of sand castles) and return to the sea. Thus all elements of the conflicting interpretations are coalesced in one scene. The naturalness of the men in relating to the wardrobe and the environment of the film suggests that what they do is real within the world of the work. Their return to the sea suggests a fantasy. Their carrying the wardrobe across the highly ordered landscape may indicate a symbolic interpretation (nonconformity in a world where conformity predominates—in the town and on the child's ordered landscape of sand castles). All of these interpretations, having equal force, leave the viewer unable to choose. Thus, many of the surrealist's favorite devices—transformations and juxtapositions, chance and coincidental occurrences, and questionable identity—work to create the characteristic uncertainty affect.

Identity and the Surreal

Making problematic the reality or unreality of a character has often been the locus of the surreal in cinema.

The Magician

Ingmar Bergman's most strikingly surrealistic film is *The Magician* (1960). During the film, the traveling magician Vogler and his troupe undergo a series of identity changes that leave the viewer uncertain whether the members of the troupe are to be regarded simply as rather inept performers of "magic" or as possessors of real magical power.

Town leaders demand a performance by Vogler and his performers. The townspeople (and we) see through Vogler's embarrassingly transparent illusions, and we think of the troupe as ordinary people who rely on illusion to perform their magical tricks.

Shortly after we settle into this identification of the troupe, a startling scene occurs. A doctor prepares to perform an autopsy on the body of Vogler, whom he has pronounced dead. As the doctor begins his work, he sees Vogler's face in a mirror. His glasses fall and are crushed, leaving him virtually sightless and helpless. The door to a grandfather clock opens—seemingly by itself. Again Vogler's image appears reflected in a mirror, which then shatters. The doctor is choked by a hand which grasps him from behind. He tries to escape. The sequence culminates with a shot (from the doctor's point of view) of Vogler staring down into his face.

The treatment of Vogler throughout the film raises questions about his identity. When he is first introduced, Vogler is supposed to be a mute. Later we find out that he can and does speak. His appearance is deceptive as well. In an especially striking scene, Vogler peels off layer after layer of his appearance, revealing that he has been wearing a false beard and a wig.

Others of Vogler's troupe have deceptive appearances. Well into the film, Mr. Aman, Vogler's young male companion, is revealed to be a woman (Ingrid Thulin) and, in fact, Vogler's wife. When her womanly identity is revealed, her long blond hair—after we have become accustomed to the short black wig of "Mr. Aman"—makes a stunning image.

Tubal, the driver of the troupe, is also deceptive, but in a literal, superficial way—as his manner, in his flirtations with the town girls, makes clear.

The Magician, *1960. Courtesy Janus Films*

An old woman in the troupe who plays the role of a witch claims that the coachman is a murderer and that he will hang himself. When her prediction comes true, the audience must question its belief that those who act fraudulent are frauds.

Deceptive appearance is not unique to members of the magical troupe. The townspeople are introduced as authority figures, but we come to regard them as fakes as well. The police chief is revealed to be a fool. The doctor maintains his pretense of supreme confidence, even after he has been reduced to complete terror in the autopsy scene.

Throughout the film the audience is confronted with reversals. It seems that it is not just the characters that are spurious, but events as well. One such reversal takes place early in the film when, after we are given the impression that one of the troupe's members has died, he reappears—only to return to his coffin and die. In another, a townsman overhears his wife seduce Vogler, but the man who comes to his wife's room is not Vogler, as we expect, but the man himself. Vogler *is* there, however—listening, but unseen. Vogler again listens and watches unseen later in the film as Ingrid (Thulin), in reaction to the doctor's discovery of her identity as Vogler's wife, tells him, "We are fakes through and through." The incidents where characters are revealed to be listening and watching events while remaining unseen suggests that there may be more to the reality of the film than we had been led to believe. (We see how incomplete each character's vision of what is taking place is.)

The final shots of the film complete the process, leaving the audience thoroughly confused as to its reality. As the troupe leaves town to give a command performance before the King, the tone of the film suddenly changes from the overbearing, ominous one that prevailed to this point to a happy one. The town becomes bathed in sunshine, and the audience is left with a traditional happy ending that seems, however, unmotivated. The audience is once again confused by the conflicting situations that the film calls upon it to accept.

Death in Venice

In Visconti's *Death in Venice* (see page 21) death figures are vehicles for the expression of surreal qualities. These figures are real characters who are connected with death in that they embody certain of its features. (The viewer cannot be certain that they are Death, unlike the case of the figure of Death in *The Seventh Seal,* who, though perceived as *unreal,* is Death.)

One of these death figures is an old man, heavily made up and dressed to appear young (in a yellowish suit, red cravat, and rakish panama), who obnoxiously accosts Aschenbach at the boat landing on his arrival in Italy. Another death figure is a gondolier who arrogantly ignores Aschenbach's directions, saying, "The Signore wants to go to the Lido."

Later, a grotesque, toothless street musician entertains the guests at Aschenbach's hotel on the Lido. He is a reminder that there have been intimations that a disease imperils Venice and with it, the plans of the tourists.

The presence of features representing Death in the old man, the boatman, and the street musician are all explicable as natural events. However, at the film's end, when Aschenbach himself assumes some of the same features, the surrealistic fabric of the film is complete. The viewer can no longer regard the embodiment of Death's features as merely natural coincidence.

To regard these features as unreal fails to account for the possibility that they can occur naturalistically. On the other hand, to regard them as realistic would in many ways contradict what we believe about the likelihood of the existence of such features. The surrealism of *Death in Venice* lies in the tension created by our sense of what is possible and what impossible.

Death in Venice, *1971*

In Renoir's *The Rules of the Game* (1939) a minor character, Berthelin, dresses in a death costume. Berthelin and his costume take on an ominous significance when an accidental death occurs.

When the character first dons the death costume, the viewer does not think of him as actually connected with death. The introduction of some real association with death comes only when fate seems so clearly to determine the so-called accidental death.

Renoir's film does not provide any hint about how to view Berthelin, and the audience again experiences the uncertainty that typically marks surreal characterizations.

The Rules of the Game, *1939. Courtesy Janus Films*

Conclusion

The source of cinematic surrealism is not to be located in the unreal, in some higher reality, or in a particular visual style. It has its locus in a distinctive reaction of the audience to what they see and hear—uncertainty whether what they perceive is to be taken as real or unreal. This occurs where a film's events are such that neither external nor internal beliefs can give the audience assurance as to how to regard them.

This uncertainty affect can be evoked in various ways. Sometimes events easily regarded as real will change their character abruptly. At other times, the viewer is uncertain throughout. An audience's experience plays a considerable role in determining how successful the uncertainty affect is. As a result, many surreal features of film are dependent upon the times in which they are viewed for their very existence.

anatomy of film criticism

PART
THREE

PART
THREE

PAR
THR

P
TH

In this final part of the book, the focus shifts from the nature of the film medium and film reality to what the film critic does with the finished film product. Critics perform certain functions that enhance our appreciation of motion pictures. One of these critical activities is that of describing the visual and aural elements and the affects of films. Much of the discussion above has dealt with such filmic description.

To round out an understanding of this process, another aspect of description—that of describing a film's style—will now be discussed. With the concept of critical description in hand, other critical activities—interpretation, determining the aesthetic qualities of films, and evaluating their success or failure—can be identified and analyzed. These further tasks of the film critic, which will also be discussed, will be seen to build upon the descriptive level.

This Part closes with some suggestions about future directions of film criticism and studies of the film medium.

cinematic styles

Realism and Expressionism

Early Developments

From its beginnings film has had discernible styles. To grasp a filmmaker's style is to gain an appreciation of the forms he uses in his portrayal of the events of his films. The styles of early films tended to be classifiable as either *realism* or *expressionism.* Louis Lumière used a realist style. In the 1890s he recorded action taking place in the world with a stationary camera. The content of his films was not unlike what we would now find in home movies—family activity *(Feeding Baby)* or activity in the streets *(Workers Leaving the Lumière Factory).* He also staged action, as in *L'Arroseur Arrosé,* in which a gardener is drenched with water by a boy.

The opposing expressionist style is found in the motion pictures created by Georges Méliès, a professional magician. Instead of recording actual

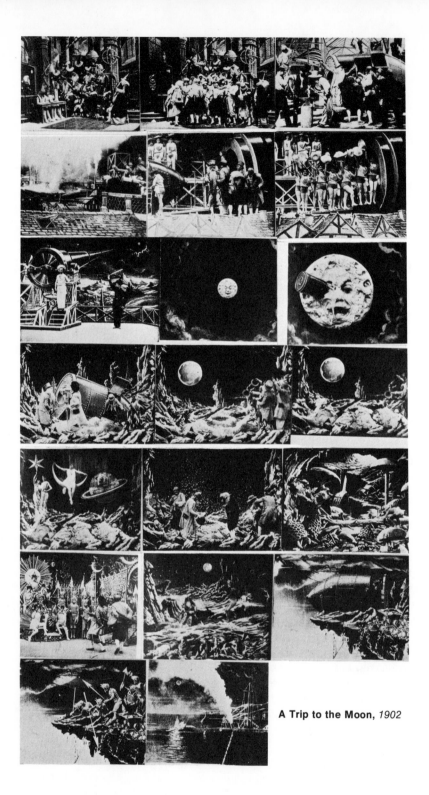

A Trip to the Moon, *1902*

events or staging real-life situations, the Méliès film sought to create something fascinating in itself. In his *The Conjuror* (1899) one sees a series of magical transformations. A magician (Méliès) and his assistant vanish. The magician becomes the assistant and, after first turning into snow, she becomes the magician. His most famous film, *A Trip to the Moon* (1902), is a fantasy about space travel with many humorous touches: The spaceship lands in the eye of the man in the moon; the moon creatures go up in smoke when the spaceship scientists hit them with their umbrellas; and planets spin around the heads of the scientists as they sleep.

Later Developments

Since these early developments the realist style has proliferated into many derivative styles: impressionism, objectivist documentary, certain other realist movements such as German realism and the New British realism, and naturalism. A key element in the impressionist style (which derives from impressionist painting) is the aim to capture the momentary and surface character of things, events, and actions. Notable examples of impressionist films are Kenji Mizoguchi's *Ugetsu Monogatari* (1953), Ophuls' *Lola Montez* (1955), Bogdanovich's *The Last Picture Show,* and Widerberg's *Elvira Madigan.* Objectivist documentary films attempt to capture the look, sounds, and feel of actual events while remaining uninvolved and as unnoticeable as possible. The documentaries of Robert Flaherty, including *The Louisiana Story* (1948) and *Nanook of the North* (1922), are among the finest in this genre. Among the most notable of other movements with a realist cast were German realism of the late 1920s—seen in films such as F. W. Murnau's *Sunrise* (1927) and *The Last Laugh* (1924), and Georg Pabst's *The Love of Jeanne Ney* (1927)—and the New British realism of the 1950s, represented by such films as Jack Clayton's *Room at the Top* (1958) and Tony Richardson's *Look Back in Anger* (1958). Films falling under the rubric of naturalism emphasize the harsh side of things and depict events in an extreme form of concrete detail. Westerns such as Sam Peckinpah's *The Wild Bunch* (1970) and *Ride the High Country* (1961) are examples of naturalism, as are John Cassavetes' *Husbands* (1971) and *Faces* (1969), Henri-Georges Clouzot's *The Wages of Fear* (1952), Carl Forman's *The Victors* (1962), and Kon Ichikawa's *Fires on the Plain* (1960).

Expressionist in style are such films as the comedies of the Marx Brothers, Chaplin, Keaton, Lubitsch, and Clair; the horror movies of Roger Corman, James Whale, and Tod Browning; and the abstract documentaries of Ruttman *(Berlin)* and Lang *(Metropolis).* Also included are films of the German expressionists of the teens and twenties, and the American film noir (thrillers such as those starring Humphrey Bogart).

Period Style and Type Style

Styles can be subdivided into *period style* and *type style.* A period style is a style or movement that is so dominant during a particular time that the whole of that time takes its name. German expressionism was such a period style. It dominated the art scene of the early 1920s in film (such as *The Cabinet of Dr. Caligari, The Golem, Nosferatu*), drama (of Meyerhold, Brecht), painting (by Munch, Kollwitz, Kandinsky, Grosz), music (Berg), and literature (Kafka). The late 1920s saw German filmmakers turning to a realist style—German realism—promulgated primarily by Murnau and Pabst.

Type style is a recurring one that may appear at any time. Expressionism and realism are examples of type styles. Lumière and Méliès represent pure cases of the realist and expressionist tendencies. Most other films are mixtures of these features, which makes specification of their styles difficult.

In determining either period style or type style, it is important to recognize that one cannot give *definitions* of style terms like "expressionist" or "realist." A definition specifies the *essence* of a thing. A circle, we can say, is a closed plane figure every point on the circumference of which is equidistant from a point called the center. The ideal of a rigorous definition is appropriate to an exact discipline such as plane geometry. However, for an inexact enterprise such as a history of film, a more flexible, less rigid form is appropriate. No feature or group of features will *always* be found in films with expressionist style, realist style, or any other style. In fact, there is no one feature (of those that count toward a judgment that a particular film is, for example, expressionist) that need be present in a film for it to be capable of being so designated. What *does* determine the designation is the presence of a sufficient number of the expressionist-making features. While the notion of a sufficient number is admittedly vague, the flexibility that style concepts need is enhanced by this vagueness. For most film historians the presence of most (or sometimes just a majority) of such expressionist-making features would warrant *expressionist*.

Weighting of features is also a factor since some features are more important at certain times than others. Our interests, our practical concerns, and the type of historical inquiry being undertaken influence weightings. For a social historian of art, features having to do with the relationships of a film to the society in which it was made would be given more weight than the visual elements used. The reverse would be true for an historian of the craft of filmmaking, who would be concerned with what the film represented in terms of the development of technique.

Finally, style concepts for film should be viewed as time-relative. With changes in the medium and in historical inquiry, the list of style determinants can be expected to change. There is thus a certain open character to the set of features that cause a film to belong to a style.[1] The set is never complete or closed to revision.

The following discussion of how this model of style concepts functions deals with films of the expressionist style.

[1] Ludwig Wittgenstein is the primary source for this model of style concepts. See his *Blue Book* (Oxford: B. Blackwell, 1958), pp. 1–30.

Exemplars of Expressionism

The Cabinet of Dr. Caligari

Robert Wiene's *The Cabinet of Dr. Caligari* (1919), a classic of the German expressionist movement, has many of the features that film historians would consider characteristic of this style. In fact, *Caligari* is the kind of pure instance of a style that we do not ordinarily find; that is, it exemplifies far more than a majority of the expressionist-making features.

In *Caligari,* distortion of forms gives concrete embodiment to a character's distortions of mind as well as to the distortions of the German culture of the time. Both interiors and exteriors lose their normal rectangularity; roofs slant at particularly sharp angles, window panes are crooked, walls slope away dangerously, trees along a road are twisted and abstract. Light, harsh and flaring, comes from strange angles, contributing to the bizarre quality.

Expressionist film utilizes a subjective rather than an objective camera. This shooting style involves showing a scene from a character's point of view rather than from a neutral standpoint. In the main, *Caligari* is shot from such a subjective standpoint. Apart from its beginning and end, the film recounts a story told by one of its characters; moreover, the events of this story are shown as they are shaped by his consciousness. The beginning and end of the film are objective camera depictions of the story-telling character, Francis, as he starts and finishes his tale.

The story he tells has an ambiguous status: It may be self-delusion or it may be fact. He reports that a certain Dr. Caligari and a man named Cesare, who performed at a local fair, murdered his friend, Alan, and the town clerk. Cesare then kidnaped Jane, Francis' fiancée. Francis followed Caligari to a mental institution, where he discovered that Caligari was a doctor who believed that he could achieve power over others through murders committed by Cesare. When he discovered that Cesare was dead, Caligari went insane, ending in confinement at the same mental institution where he had been a doctor.

During the ending, Francis is shown as an inmate telling the story to another inmate in the mental institution. Jane and Cesare are inmates also, and Caligari is its director. Francis becomes violent and is led away under the care of a seemingly benevolent Caligari.

This ending supposedly shows that Francis' story was an invention of his twisted mind. It is difficult, however, for us to accept that Caligari is benevolent, Francis mad, and that all we have seen is Francis' fantasy—especially since the final scene displays the same visual distortions that characterized Francis' story. If the final scene gives the true view of things, of course, it should not possess these distortions. The film, however, can be interpreted as a revolutionary document, in which case Francis' vision is correct regarding Caligari's inner nature.[2] Thus Caligari stands for authority in the society in which the film

[2] Siegfried Kracauer, *From Caligari to Hitler* (Princeton, N.J.: Princeton University Press, 1947), pp. 70–71.

The Cabinet of Dr. Caligari, *1919*

is made, and the film is an indictment of an authoritarian Germany. In this interpretation, the ending, in which Francis is depicted as mad (thus denying the tyrannical nature of authority by making Francis' story a fantasy) is analogous to what was taking place in German society of the time, in which outwardly respectable forms masked tyrannical impulses and madness.

Expressionism emphasizes atmosphere and mood rather than concrete detail. In *Caligari,* gothic forms, jagged lines, dark sets, and painted shadows create an ominous atmosphere.

Having a theme centering on alienation is also an expressionist feature. If the events depicted are filtered through the madness of a character, then the substance of our experience of *Caligari* is of an alienated consciousness of events and environment.

The stream-of-consciousness technique can be an expressionist mode of representation. In *Caligari,* events and actions are fragments of memory, dreams, fantasy, nightmares, and symbolic thoughts in Francis' stream of consciousness. Most notable is the scene in which Caligari fantasizes about gaining the mythic powers of an ancestral namesake. The words "Caligari" and "I must be Caligari" literally appear on the environment. Moreover, the whole of Francis' story is a nightmare, containing the symbolic thought that authority is mad. The character *Dr. Caligari* is the vehicle for this symbolism. Also, as discussed above, it is unclear how much of Francis' consciousness of events is reality and how much fantasy and symbolic thoughts.

Expressionist *mise en scène* is marked by a high degree of stylization and exaggeration. In *Caligari,* setting, acting, make-up, and costume embody these qualities. The basis of their use in the film is essentially the conflict of opposites. The appearance of Francis' fiancée and of Cesare are alike in that each embodies visual contrast. Their faces are eerily white, while Cesare's leotard and Jane's eyes and hair are starkly black.

Sets contrast from time to time as well. Against the many scenes (described above) emphasizing sharp-edged, angular lines, are set scenes organized around circular patterns. Jane's room conveys an appearance of security by its markedly circular shape.[3] We also see many circular patterns at the fair, including that arising from the irising used in that scene. Although the circular patterns at the fair leave us comparatively at ease, there remains the underlying feeling of horror established by the generally unstable environment of the film.

The conflict of opposites supports the theme of ambiguity. The opposites must be reconciled in order for us to understand the action. While the existence of opposites in the film permits various interpretations, one's own interpretation is generally determined by the way in which one understands the ending in relation to Francis' story.

As a classic of expressionist style, *The Cabinet of Dr. Caligari* exerted the most profound influence upon what expressionism in film would become. Films made in the style subsequently have been built upon the core of features found in *Caligari,* with different contexts found for their use and sometimes with the expressionist features expanded.

---

[3] See Marsha Kinder and Beverle Houston, *Close-Up: A Critical Perspective on Film* (New York: Harcourt Brace Jovanovich, 1972), pp. 26–30, for a useful analysis of the film's structure.

Last Year at Marienbad

Alain Resnais' *Last Year at Marienbad* (1961) possesses many expressionist qualities. It is one long stream of consciousness, showing everything from the viewpoint of a character. The interior of the baroque-style hotel in which the action of the film occurs is shaped by the character's feelings.

A fundamental aspect of *Marienbad's* form is the interaction of two concurrent time phases. In one, all of the events in the film can be considered to be *in* the present in that what we see and hear during the ninety-three minutes of the film is occurring in the consciousness of one character, that of the lover. The sequences of the film are comprised of the lover's perceptions, memories, and fantasies as he moves about the hotel (identified in the film as being in Frederiksbad), thinking back on events (centering on his relationship with a woman) that occurred during his previous visit there. In addition, the lover recalls (or partly fantasizes) a prior meeting with the woman at Marienbad that occurred exactly one year prior to the first visit to Frederiksbad.

Viewed in terms of the other time phase, not all of the film's events are *of* or *about* the present. Most of the contents of the lover's consciousness have reference to the past. Some of his awarenesses are, to be sure, perceptions of the hotel as he walks through it, but these perceptions constitute only a small portion of the totality of *Last Year at Marienbad.*

Thus, a given shot or sequence of shots can be regarded from either of two temporal viewpoints: either as *in* the present (that is, in the mind of the lover) or *of* the present (if a perception) or *of* the past (if a memory/fantasy of what he experienced at Frederiksbad and Marienbad).

Examples of the present being perceived are the opening prologue (as the lover moves through the hotel noticing and remarking upon its qualities), the closing shot of the hotel from a distance, and a sequence at night in which the camera tracks through the empty hotel and gardens. The remaining sequences deal with the lover's attempts to restructure what happened at Frederiksbad and at Marienbad in order to expiate feelings of guilt about his part in those events.

The following description of a sequence composed of the lover's stream of consciousness indicates its typical expressionist content of fantasy, memory, nightmare, and symbolic thoughts.

The woman has been shot by her companion. As she falls, her finger is over her lips as when one cautions another to be silent. This gesture indicates the close connection between discretion and the basic structure of the lover's stream of consciousness. He was not present at the shooting, but he imagines that the woman cautioned him to keep the secret of their affair even at her death. The lover believes that his responsibility in the affair obliges him to conceal it from her companion. He persuades himself that he could not have been expected to break off the relationship, by dwelling throughout upon its obsessive qualities, much like those involved in his playing of the match game.

The lover remembers or imagines that he fulfilled his responsibility by such actions as sitting at a table separate from hers in a restaurant, and leaving the patio by going over the balustrade when the woman saw her companion coming. (She urged him to leave "if you love me.")

If the lover can persuade himself that he was not fully responsible for the initiation and continuation of the affair with the woman, and that *he exercised full discretion,* then he will have accomplished his objective in entertaining the stream of consciousness that constitutes the film—he will have expiated his feeling of guilt about his role in the woman's death. (Alain Resnais says that if he were to sum up his film in one word, he would choose "persuasion.")

The lover then remembers or imagines a set of circumstances at Marienbad that implicate the woman in the initiation of the affair, and he remembers or imagines a set of events at Frederiksbad, some indefinite time ago, that indicate the woman's participation in the continuation of the affair.

He is conscious that in Marienbad the woman left her bedroom door open so that he could gain admission. It, thus, only *appeared* that a rape occurred, he persuades himself, since the woman really wanted him.

As the lover finds himself being rushed down the brightly lit corridor in Frederiksbad, toward the woman's room and her welcoming arms, he remarks, as narrator, in a violent tone: "No, No, No, that's wrong. It wasn't by force . . . Remember . . . For days and days, every night. . . . All the rooms look alike. . . . But that room, for me didn't look like any other. . . . There were no more doors."

In another scene, this one in a garden at Frederiksbad, the lover remarks, "You are on the point of leaving. The door of your room is still open." He continues to persuade himself of his innocence in a scene where the woman is sitting alone on the bed in her hotel room. Here the lover's voice is heard, "At that hour, in any case, he [the companion] is at the gambling table. I had warned you I would come. You didn't answer. When I came, I found all the doors ajar; the door to the vestibule of your apartment, the door of the little sitting room, the door to your bedroom—I had only to push them open. . . ."

In other parts of the film, the lover tries to remember the sequence of events in the woman's bedroom at Marienbad. He searches for the pattern of the woman's actions in that room. Did she leave the door open? Did she fall on the bed from the left side or the right? How did she look? (The image flickers several times as he struggles to remember.) He also thinks of the woman as having been shot by her companion in the same feathered garments that she wore when he was rushed down the brightly lit halls into her arms. This costume is recognized by the lover as the attire of seduction. In the script, Robbe-Grillet instructs that the woman should fall (after being shot by the companion) in an openly provocative manner across the bed. This is accomplished by having the feathered dress come half open as she falls. Thus, the lover's consciousness of the scenes in Marienbad is such that he implicates the woman in the initiation of the affair.

To convince himself that the woman also shared in the continuation of the affair, the lover focuses his attention on the ways in which she appeared to dissimulate her feelings for him. For example, she planned accidental meetings with him. In the scene where the woman moves alone despondently through the garden in Frederiksbad, the lover narrates about how they met, "You still avoided meeting my eyes. Apparently you were doing it on purpose—systematically."

In the hotel's salon, they sit at separate tables and the lover remarks, "You never seemed to be waiting for me—but we kept meeting at each turn of the paths—behind each bush, at the foot of each statue, near each pond." She seemed to be aloof, yet she was arranging their encounters in Frederiksbad. Thus, even though he remembers that he constantly attempted to make her remember the affair they had had in Marienbad (and thereby that he had participated in the process of continuing the affair), he remembers or imagines that she also played a role in the continuation of the affair.

The lover accomplishes the second persuasion (that he exercised as much discretion as was humanly possible) by remembering or imagining that her companion had seen them together in the garden only by accident. The lover remembers having gone over the balustrade following the woman's exhortation to do so "if you love me." The lover is then conscious of the companion coming down the walk toward the woman. Just after the lover goes over the balustrade, a loud sound is heard. A little later in the lover's stream of consciousness, we see that the balustrade is broken. The lover convinces himself that the accidental breaking of the balustrade is the only way the companion discovered his existence. Having convinced himself that he tried to leave unnoticed, the lover will have assuaged, to some extent, his feelings of responsibility for the woman's death.

An indication of how the lover sees his role and that of the companion in the killing of the woman is revealed in the film's two shooting-gallery scenes. In the first, the companion is standing with a group of men who are prepared to fire. As the companion's time to shoot comes, he turns to fire at the targets. Not only do we hear his firing but we see that he hits the target. On the other hand, when it is the lover's time to shoot, he is able only to turn to fire; he is not able to fire (no sound is heard). Also, the scene with the companion on the firing line follows a scene where the woman and the lover are alone in the woman's bedroom. This bedroom scene ends with the woman screaming, the sound of her scream masked by the first of the pistol detonations from the range.

In his final awareness, the lover has gained some measure of distance from the events that have been occupying his consciousness for an hour and a half. He has given the events a desired pattern—that is, he has persuaded himself that there are grounds for mitigating his feeling of guilt about the murder of the woman. The lover's distance toward what has occurred in the past is symbolized by the film's last shot, in which, for the first time, we see the hotel from a distance.

Five Easy Pieces

Bob Rafelson's *Five Easy Pieces* (1970) is the story of the black sheep in a successful and artistic family. The main character, Bob (Jack Nicholson), has turned his back on his upper-class background to become a drifter. When the film opens he is working in a California oil field. When things go awry at the oil fields, he returns home to become entangled in all the old family conflicts that had originally driven him away. He tells his paralyzed father, in a poignant monologue, that he always moves on before things go bad, and he does not stay at the family home long.

The environments and personal relationships of the film are shaped by Bob's consciousness. Through most of the film, we are given a view of things from a subjective camera, with Bob's consciousness being the point of view. In the sequences in which Bob becomes dissatisfied with his life in the oil fields, he is photographed in a way that makes him appear to be an extraneous element there. For example, when he returns from a visit to his sister's recording studio,

Five Easy Pieces, *1970*

rather than seeing Bob already present in his girl friend's place (as in prior scenes) we see him *entering* it—a subtle visual indication that he does not belong there.

This theme of being extraneous to the environment is continued during the sequence where Bob returns to his family home. He seems an intruder as he goes through the various stages involved in entering this world. A subjective camera again tracks with Bob as he enters and moves through the family home. Coming closer to his distant family, as he passes through door after door, he seems always to be outside going in.

A scene where Bob plays the piano is imbued with the feeling of a character, Catherine, for whom he is playing. As the camera tilt-pans over the family's musical past and associations represented in photographs that hang on the wall, the feelings of this woman, with whom he has become involved, force themselves upon Bob. Once again Bob feels stifled and controlled by another. When Bob departs again at the end of the film, the viewer thinks back to scenes like this one for explanation. It is an accumulation of oppressive, stifling experiences that seem to be at the core of Bob's alienation.

Realistic Style: Analysis by Comparison

As noted above, "realism" as a style concept occupies the other end of the style continuum from expressionism. Realism in the stylistic sense is not to be confused with the discussion of film *reality* in Chapter Five. Though there is some relationship between the two, there are significant differences. When a critic identifies a film as realist in style, she is not at the same time marking the fact that the film portrays the real. She is concerned with clusters of features such as: the actual events are portrayed faithfully; symbolism is minimal; the *mise en scène* tends to have the look and feel of everyday life; camera placement, shooting angles, and movements are rarely unusual; the impact of events in the film is greater than the audience is accustomed to experiencing in recent films; the film emphasizes concrete detail. Whether possession of these realist features makes for a capturing of the real is problematic. Sometimes it may; other times it will not. Furthermore, highly expressionistic images, as in the case of *Sanjuro, October,* or *Death in Venice* (see Chapter Five), can portray reality eminently well.

The following analysis of how the same subject is treated with expressionist and realist styles governing the portrayal delineates the differences between these two approaches.

The Story of Joan of Arc

An Expressionist Version   Carl Dreyer's *The Passion of Joan of Arc* (1928), a silent-film classic made in France, provides a re-creation of the arrest, interrogation, trial, and conviction of the famous historical figure who was memorialized as a saint after her death. In his treatment of the subject, Dreyer tends to move his camera very close in shots of Joan and the judges as they seek to gain admissions of wrongdoing from her. These close-ups shape the environment of the film into one of confinement, giving visual expression to Joan's feelings about her situation. Where an impressionist (a realist category) film would dwell upon the surface features of reality, Dreyer seeks the inner, hidden feelings of the participants. Where the impressionist film would seek to capture the momentary quality of a situation, Dreyer is after universals.

His close-ups show the viewer Joan's feelings about her interrogation. For her, nothing else matters but the process she is undergoing. Hers is a universal struggle. The extreme camera position provides us with little else but a view of this process. Our attention is commanded by the huge figures before us and the spiritual struggle taking place. *Mise en scène* has the characteristic stylized quality that we associate with expressionist treatments. Showing the actors without make-up makes us vividly aware of the qualities of the protagonist and her antagonists. The ugliness of their faces contrasts with the glow that emanates from Joan's. The coldness of the setting contrasts with her inner character as well. The forces of good and evil are distinguished by light and dark in many scenes where Joan's countenance contrasts with the gloomy surroundings. Clothes also exhibit this thematic contrast.

Shooting angle and camera movement make the environment expressive of the characters' feelings. During the interrogations, the camera pans over the judges' faces, coming to rest in a static shot of joan's face. The shots of the judges' faces are from Joan's point of view, as they encircle her. The static views of Joan are expressive of the judges' perspective: They see her as trapped.

During those scenes where Joan is indecisive, she is seen by the subjective camera from a high angle, which makes her look insignificant relative to the judges, who are made domineering by a low shooting angle. This pattern is reversed in later scenes when Joan has resolved to die for her faith. She is now the imposing figure seen from a low angle.

Near the end, when Joan has made her decision, editing rhythms quicken, in contrast to the slow pace that has marked earlier scenes. This alteration in tempo indicates the closeness of death and the imminent end of *The Passion of Joan of Arc.*

The Realist Version   Robert Bresson's cinematic portrayal of the story of Joan of Arc—*The Trial of Joan of Arc* (1961)—in contrast to that of Dreyer, tends toward the realist pole in style. In his depiction of the struggle between Joan and her captors, Bresson permits himself little contrast in lighting. Unlike the case in Dreyer's film, where good and evil are symbolized by patterns of light and dark, the main tone in Bresson's treatment is grey. There is indeed very little symbolism in the film. Bresson prefers to give a straightforward recounting of the story, remaining as faithful as possible to the historical record of the trial. In the trial room, the camera shows only the person speaking. There are no extreme shooting angles as in Dreyer's film. The interrogator is always photographed straight on, with no variation in shooting angle.

With Bresson's use of nonprofessional actors, his emphasis on historical dialogue over image, and the simplicity of the style, noted above, the film seems almost to tend toward an objectivist documentary style. There are, however, other elements of style at work. The dialogue, composed of incessant questions and answers, is coordinated into a complex texture of rhythms that are related to the larger structure of the film by their connection with natural sounds (footsteps, doors opening and closing, locks being turned).

critical
interpretation

As we have seen, the first level of critical treatment is that of describing a film's visual, aural, and affective properties. Building upon this descriptive level, the critic next offers interpretations of the film. Under the interpretive eye of the critic, films are seen as expressive of such things as religious truths, mythic ideas, humanistic themes, and universal symbols.

With descriptions and interpretations formulated, the critic can then identify the aesthetic qualities of the film (the third level). Determining aesthetic qualities (unity, disunity, humor, intensity, drama) presupposes descriptive and interpretive activity. Films have aesthetic qualities because of the relations among their visual elements, sound, and affects (first level) and because of an overlying concept that structures them, such as a theme or mythic idea (second level).

Finally, at the fourth level, passing a verdict on or evaluating a film is the critical act of deciding that it is aesthetically good or bad. Such verdicts are dependent primarily on third-level aesthetic judgments.

While first-level criticism remains relatively unproblematic, that at the second level has been called into question at one time or another. One of the most articulate expressions of such dissatisfaction comes from Susan Sontag, particularly in her essay *Against Interpretation.*[1]

It is Sontag's belief that critical interpretation all too often leads the would-be appreciator of art in general and of film in particular away from rather than into the work of art. She cites D. H. Lawrence's motto, "Never trust the teller, trust the tale," and sees the tendency to seek meanings behind what is *literally* before us in the work of art as symptomatic of a desire to *control* by putting things into manageable categories.

Sontag regards the latter part of the twentieth century as a time when there is an especially acute need to have direct contact with things. Our world shows an impoverishment of communication on a literal level and of connection with living, unmanageable things. Art, however, can be a vehicle of the literal and the unmanageable.

Some of the finest artists have, nevertheless, been subjected to unceasing interpretation. Kafka's character K in *The Trial* has been viewed as a Christ figure or an anti-Christ, as both and as neither. Sontag notes that "Beckett's delicate dramas of the withdrawn consciousness are read as a statement about modern man's alienation from meaning or from God, or as an allegory of psychopathology."[2] She points out that Tennessee Williams' play *A Streetcar Named Desire* is viewed as a portrayal of the "decline of Western civilization . . . [instead of] a play about a handsome brute named Stanley Kowalski and a faded, mangy belle named Blanche Du Bois."[3]

Sontag points to much of modern art as a process of creating works that are "flights from interpretation." Symbol-hunting interpretive excess is difficult with painting that has no content. Pop art achieves a similar objective in opposite fashion, presenting so obvious content (for example, Andy Warhol's giant *Campbell's Soup Can*) that it is uninterpretable. In cinema, Sontag admires the works of Warhol, Godard, and Truffaut for their "anti-symbolic quality." The value of antisymbolism, then, is its ability to bring us closer to art itself: There are no symbolic interpretations available to interfere with our experience.

Stanley Kubrick's *A Clockwork Orange* (1971) can be understood in many significant ways in terms of the antisymbolic dynamic that Sontag discusses. The main character, Alex, is in contact with his feelings. His violence is not a

---

[1] The explication of Sontag's views that follows is based upon her essay "Against Interpretation," which is included in her book *Against Interpretation and Other Essays* (New York: Dell, 1961), pp 13–24.
[2] Ibid., p. 18.
[3] Ibid.

product of some underlying neurosis. He does violent things because he likes to, because it is fun, because it is exciting and vital.

One of the more shocking scenes in *Clockwork* is Alex's murder of a woman with her own work of art—a huge sculpture of a human penis, which is so obviously the male sexual organ that it cannot be symbolic. The pop art in *Clockwork* is of the antisymbolic style. In this world, fantasy is no longer distinguishable from experience, art from life.

The slow pace of Kubrick's film, sharply criticized by many commentators, gives us time to see all the pop art in the film's environments. As Sontag observes, we live such a fast, cluttered life that we need time and literal substance to regain our sensitivities. *Clockwork* gives us both.

How valid is Sontag's argument? It may be granted that some interpretations are artificially imposed on the works they are meant to illuminate. Seeing *A Streetcar Named Desire* as a portrayal of the decline of Western civilization seems an obvious case of such overinterpretation. It may also be admitted that much modern art, including contemporary film, possesses an antiinterpretive or antisymbolic aspect. The example of *Clockwork* brings out the value of this perspective. The question remains, however, whether film is better appreciated without interpretation.

Sontag's argument rests on the notion that perceiving a film while having an interpretation in mind interferes with perceiving the literal content of the film. The moviegoer is supposedly faced with a choice of ways to appreciate a film— ways that Sontag alleges are mutually exclusive. Sontag would emphasize the descriptive level of appreciation while avoiding, as much as possible, the interpretive level. Interpretation, however, does not always (or even frequently) interfere with grasping what is literally in the film. Instead, it often happens that the two modes of awareness—one literal, the other interpretive—arise together.

In *Clockwork Orange,* for instance, a viewer can be aware of both the descriptive-level features of the film *and* the interpretive structures. One interpretation is based on the idea of catharsis—of the subconscious gaining release: The audience identifies with Alex, who, throughout the film is treated as a more attractive character than the stereotypic figures around him.[4] His engaging dialogue, his wit, his running narrative, and his daring compare favorably with the characters of the fascist guard, the overplayed liberal, Alex's sappy parents, his sidekicks (who become police), and so on. In this identification, the audience resents the stifling of Alex.

In the workings of the subconscious, persons and situations become exaggerated, hence the stereotyping and simplified forms of conflict in *Clockwork.* The distortions of the environment, the fast- and slow-motion fantasies, and the nightmare quality of the Ludovico Centre treatment sequences (with their

---

[4] From an interview with Stanley Kubrick that appeared in *Saturday Review,* December 25, 1971.

reverberations of the subconscious) serve to create an atmosphere where this cartharsis can take place.

Mythic narrative structures may also be found in *Clockwork*. Alex's adventure has been viewed as a kind of odyssey, complete with a return to a place marked "Home." The celebration that follows Alex's recovery from the Ludovico treatment (which takes away inclinations toward violence) reaffirms his humanity by expressing the mythic idea that violence and combat are natural to the human condition.

La Strada (1954) by Federico Fellini is another film that may be fruitfully discussed in terms of the issue of interpretation. It is the story of a strongman, Zampano, who is so cruelly indifferent to his pathetic companion-assistant that he seems incapable of human feeling. But, in the closing sequence when he realizes that she is irretrievably gone, he feels his loss deeply.

La Strada is, as the title implies, a song of the road. One responds to the naturalistic atmosphere of the film, the damp roads, squalor, meager meals, and a feeling of hopelessness and emptiness. This response does not involve interpretation. The experience of viewing *La Strada* can, however, be enriched by symbolic analysis.

In Fellini's world, characters are condemned to solitude. Their attempts to escape this condition lead them to involve themselves in collective celebrations. These celebrations include a circus *(The Clowns)*, an orgy *(La Dolce Vita)*, a procession *(8½)*, a masquerade *(Juliet of the Spirits)*, and a feast *(Fellini's Satyricon)*. After this escape attempt has spent itself, the characters find themselves all the more solitary. Dawn is usually the moment when the illusion of escape is dissipated and the characters return to their aloneness.

In *La Strada*, Gelsomina seeks fellowship through her singing and dancing, in order to overcome her feelings of homesickness. Zampano rejects her, leaving her in the condition of aloneness. In the end, Fellini leaves Zampano in the same condition, and we are painfully aware of his isolation.

Gelsomina's and Zampano's relationship to Il Matto, the tightrope walker, is structured on the symbolic idea of a balance in nature between the primal forces of fire (associated with Zampano) and water (associated with Gelsomina). When we first see Il Matto, he is shown walking a tightrope through a veil of flame. In a later scene, in which he and Zampano fight, Il Matto attacks Zampano with water. Still later, Zampano tries to conceal his accidental killing of Il Matto by pushing his car off an embankment into a river bed. Fire appears again as the car erupts into flames. Il Matto balances between the two primitive elements of nature and the two characters associated with them.

The odd relationship Il Matto attempts with Gelsomina is understandable in terms of this underlying archetypal structure. He asks her to go with him, then says he will not have her. He urges her to leave Zampano, then agrees that she ought to stay. The natural balance he tries to accomplish is one that can only lead to this kind of ambivalence.

Thus central aspects of the relationships in *La Strada* require a symbolic interpretation. As in the case of the appreciation of *Clockwork*, the viewer need not make a choice between two modes of response: One enriches the other.

In light of the examples from *A Clockwork Orange* and *La Strada,* it would seem that Sontag's viewpoint needs modification: While the symbolic should not be the sole mode of perception of a film, it and the literal mode of perception are not incompatible.

Interpretation, then, can add to and thereby enrich our experience of motion pictures; the forms that this mode of critical activity takes will be clarified below.

The Mythically Grounded Film

An important aspect of many films is the presence of mythic structures. Characters, objects, and events in film can not only be *physically* bigger than corresponding elements in real life but also *thematically* larger than life (in terms of the myths they may embody). Mythic elements are important in film because of the way in which they can serve as fundamental structures in the development of action. ("Mythic" here is not used in the sense of "fictional" or "false," but rather in the sense of an embodiment of a final and significant belief of a culture.)

The mythic has taken many forms. In the ancient world, mythic stories concerned gods or other supernatural beings or extraordinary events. Over the course of history, secularized forms of these myths developed that involved persons or events of everyday existence.

Myths play a structural role in all genres of film: the horror movie, western, gangster, thriller, detective mystery, adventure, Biblical epic, comedy, tragedy romance.

The German expressionist movement includes, in addition to *Caligari,* two prominent horror films: Paul Wegener's *The Golem* (1914, remade 1920), a Frankenstein story, and Friedrich Murnau's *Nosferatu* (1922), a Dracula story. *The Golem* is based on a Jewish legend in which a rabbi gives life to a statue made of clay (a Golem). An antique dealer receives the Golem from some workmen who excavated it at the site of an old synagogue. Using his knowledge of the rabbi's secrets, he gives life to the Golem and makes it his servant. The Golem falls in love with the dealer's daughter. When she rejects him, he becomes enraged and pursues her, destroying everything in his path.

The Golem is grounded in the Faustian myth that there is knowledge that human beings dare not seek; that there are areas of life best left unexplored because it is not in harmony with nature for the human race to possess knowledge of them. Faust seeks to go beyond the limitations of his nature by selling his soul for such knowledge. The dealer—and a host of other characters in literature (such as Dr. Frankenstein in James Whale's film *Frankenstein* (1931)—commits a crime against nature by creating life from the inanimate.

In the Frankenstein story, another myth—that love will conquer all—plays a crucial role in stopping the terrifying rampage of the monster. In the stunning final scene of Whale's film, Frankenstein, motivated by his love for his bride, overcomes the evil he has created: The image of the monster, reflected in a huge mirror, is gradually replaced by that of Frankenstein.

The structuring of their horror films on the Faust myth (and, in the case of *Frankenstein,* also on the notion that love triumphs over evil) gives a universality to the action of the Wegener and Whale films that enables them to touch us deeply.

F. W. Murnau's *Nosferatu,* like the Frankenstein story, establishes a universal base for its story by grounding it in the mythic belief in the power of love over evil. In brilliant fashion, Murnau weaves a supernatural texture into the world of his film—one threatened by Count Nosferatu's need for human blood. A young clerk, sent to the Count's castle to settle a business matter, is brought there in a coach driven by phantoms through the Carpathian Woods. The ride is given the atmosphere of the supernatural by the use of fast motion and negative image. The clerk miraculously escapes an attack by Nosferatu, and the vampire follows him, wreaking much havoc, until he is destroyed. The final scene and the one in which the clerk escapes contain archetypal significance. In the earlier one, as the vampire is about to attack the clerk, the clerk's wife, Nina, awakens in her home in a distant city sensing that her absent husband is in danger. Her concern for her beloved asserts itself over the miles and forces Nosferatu to stop his attack. In the final scene, Nina meets the vampire and, knowing that he will be destroyed if he is abroad when the sun rises, fearlessly invites him to stay the night with her. He does, and dies.

The Blue Angel and *Cabaret,* whose *mise en scène* was discussed above (see page 38), are representative of the way musicals can tap mythic sources for part of their appeal. The teacher in *The Blue Angel* is an archetypal figure involved in a struggle for nothing less than his soul. Liza Minelli in *Cabaret* talks of her ancient instincts, and her performances in the Kit Kat Club are celebrations of demoniac possession. This feature becomes especially apparent in the scene near the end where Liza and the master of ceremonies burst out of a set that resembles a kind of Hades.

The genre of the musical has rather direct connections with the mythic. Much of its power lies in the ability of musicals to serve unconscious yearnings such as we discover in our dreams. We unconsciously want to live in a world where everything is intensified (in musicals people dance instead of walking, sing instead of talking); where all is bright, sunny, and warm; and where the power of love makes everything work out well in the end.

Chaplin's comic style has also been thought of in terms of a mythical framework. André Bazin says of Chaplin's famous characterization of the little tramp: "Charlie is a mythical figure who rises above every adventure in which he becomes involved."[5] Charlie's mythical status can be traced to his ability to

---

[5] André Bazin, *What Is Cinema?,* Vol. I, translated by Hugh Gray (Berkeley: University of California Press, 1967), p. 144.

resolve all problematical situations in a way that manifests everyman's fantasies.[6] In *Modern Times* (1936) Chaplin conquers the machine age, the prison system, and the unions. Charlie's triumph over authority vicariously fulfills some of the deepest needs arising from our relation to the highly structured life of our society. We would like to be able to do what Chaplin does.

Much of the structure of the adventure dramas of Howard Hawks has mythical roots. In *Hatari* (1962) John Wayne likens to "natural process" the rivalry of several hunters over the only available woman. The mythic idea that a man must test himself against the environment and prove himself to his peers is the basis of the rituals characters undergo to become part of the inner circle in *Hatari*.

The western has one of the strongest connections with the mythic. The oppositions that make up the core of the western are grounded in archetypes concerning mankind's place in nature. The western celebrates the myth of the natural appropriateness of combat. Henry King's *The Gunfighter* (1950) attempts to depart from this structure. In it Gregory Peck plays an aging gunfighter who is weary of the life he leads. Fatally wounded by a youth who will now wear the mythic mantle of invincibility, Peck insists that the boy not be arrested but be left the worse fate of having to live with the reputation of a gunfighter. One feels that the attempt in *The Gunfighter* to counteract the traditional structure of westerns is ineffectual, perhaps because it substitutes another myth—that of the lonely superman who stoically endures the blows of a malign fate. Our attachments to the myth of the appropriateness of combat are too strong to be easily overthrown.

George Stevens' *Shane* (1953) is, in the words of one perceptive critic, the portrayal of

> the pearl-handled-gun-toting Messiah who can save the endangered land from the forces of lawlessness. . . . We see Shane (played by Alan Ladd) through the eyes of America's future, young Joey Starrett. . . . It is not by accident that Joey's parents are named Joe and Marion, standing in wait for the Messiah-son who will deliver them. . . .[7]

> The coming of the Western hero is a kind of Second Coming of Christ, but this time he wears the garb of the gunfighter, the only Savior the sagebrush, the wilderness, and the pure savagery of the West can accept.[8]

Shane does not want to fight anymore, and so some of *The Gunfighter's* structure is involved in Stevens' "morality play." But when Shane must act, he does so with great savagery. The boy's ringing celebration of Shane's name at the end of the movie reestablishes the mythic sanctity of combat.

---

[6] Chaplin's choice of heroines further exemplifies this mythic quality. They are always highly romanticized (for example, Paulette Goddard in *Modern Times*).

[7] Michael Marsden, "Savior in the Saddle," in Jack Nachbar, ed., *Focus on the Western* (Englewood Cliffs, N.J.: Prentice Hall, 1974), p. 97.

[8] Ibid., p. 95.

The mythic is not to be seen as an extraneous element in our perception of movies. We do not perceive the story of a western, for example, and then recognize its connections with mythic themes and archetypal images. The two things arise together because our very perception of the events of the story is accomplished via mythic categories.

When Wyatt Earp steps down to the OK Corral to defend the town against lawless elements in John Ford's *My Darling Clementine* (1946), his act is imbued with mythic sanctity. Operative in the audience's perception of his confrontation with the gang is the myth of "natural harmony." Part of what we see happening is, to be sure, a man facing a group of hoodlums. But another part of what we perceive is a restoration of the balance of nature. Evil, represented by the hoodlums, is present in the world, but by some natural process this force will be neutralized by the appearance of a counterforce for good, embodied, in this case, in Wyatt Earp. Countless other westerns built upon this mythic structure rely for their effectiveness on the audience perceiving the confrontation scenes partly under the category of the "natural harmony" myth.[9]

A myth can make its way from one genre to the next. In a western, the individual, facing a primitive environment, discovers his identity. He has a sidekick—often an Indian—his horse, and his gun. Evil is an essential part of that environment and, after much tribulation, is overcome.

In a gangster film, the same elements may be found. The gun is there, though it can appear in more complicated form (for example, a machine gun). The auto replaces the horse and the city becomes the substitute for the primitive environment. The heroic dimension associated with the Western hero is usually lost in this translation. Where the cowboy has authority stemming from a code of honor to which he closely conforms, the gangster has merely power.

Schlesinger's *Midnight Cowboy* is a fascinating mixture of these two forms of a mythic structure.[10] Joe Buck (Jon Voight) dresses in cowboy garb and, when in high spirits, whoops like the cowboy hero of untold westerns. The wilderness that he heads out into is New York City, his range the wealthy women of the city. The stagecoach that takes him there and then to the promised new frontier (Florida) is the Greyhound bus.

In New York Joe Buck encounters that myth-bound figure, the Indian, in the form of Rico "Ratzo" Rizzo, a crippled hustler (Dustin Hoffman). In the western, the cowboy's encounter with the primitive environment and his relationship to the Indian bring about a change in his identity. At the end of *Midnight Cowboy,* we find that Joe Buck has undergone such a transformation. On the way to Florida, he casts away his cowboy garb for an outfit appropriate to a new life in Miami and announces that he will now get a job.

---

[9] Fred Zinnemann's *High Noon* (1952) is perhaps the most notable example.
[10] This interpretation of *Midnight Cowboy* was suggested in a January 1972 lecture at the University of Southern California by Leslie Fiedler.

Midnight Cowboy, *1969*

While Joe Buck fulfills many of the features of the mythic western cowboy, he also fits the familiar role of antihero, present in many so-called "new" westerns (and other genres as well). His attempts to earn a living fail, and, when they first meet, Ratzo hustles him. Buck's failures culminate in murder and flight. The film ends with a final antiheroic note when Ratzo, whom Buck has tried to save, dies.

Despite this antiheroic element, *Midnight Cowboy* taps mythic sources. Though few will consciously think of Joe Buck as having an archetypal dimension, mythic categories nevertheless remain part of the conceptual framework that keys our response.[11]

Structuralism and Dialectic Interpretation

Another interpretive form is that of the *dialectic,* an interaction of opposing forces from which a synthesis comes. A prominent and influential theory of film interpretation called *structuralism* places great emphasis on dialectical structures in the understanding of films. Some of these structures are myths, for the mythic often rests upon oppositions.

In explaining how mythic and other dialectical structures shape our perception of film events, structuralists take the position that the world is a function of the forms our consciousness gives it.

Among the most prominent structuralists are Noel Burch, a filmmaker and film theoretician; Claude Lévi-Strauss, an anthropologist whose studies have often focused on ritual and myth; and Christian Metz, who applies the techniques of modern linguistic theory to analysis of visual and aural elements of film as cinematic signs, symbols, and other structures.[12] Structuralist approaches, from whatever field, converge in being antihistorical. The wider implications of structuralism are discussed in Chapter 10.

Peter Wollen has used the films of Howard Hawks to demonstrate how a structuralist analysis would work.[13] Instead of dwelling on the concrete details of a film or the reasons why an audience at a particular time will respond in a particular way, the structuralist seeks out so-called deep structural characteristics. In the case of Hawks' films, the focus of attention is usually certain recurrent motifs, incidents, and visual styles that arise from oppositions. Hawks is an especially interesting case because he has worked in virtually every film genre, although most of his films are of two types: the adventure drama and the crazy comedy. The highest emotion in his films of the first

---

[11] For analysis of the concept of the mythic, see Suzanne Langer, *Philosophy in a New Key* (Cambridge: Harvard University Press, 1942) and Ernst Cassirer, *Language and Myth* (New York: Harper and Brothers, 1946).

[12] Other structuralists are Ferdinand de Saussure (the father of the movement), Roman Jacobson, Roland Barthes, Umberto Eco, and Paolo Pasolini.

[13] The following explanation of structural characteristics in Hawks' films is from the presentation made by Peter Wollen in his *Signs and Meaning in the Cinema* (Bloomington: Indiana University Press, 1969), pp. 80–94.

type is the camaraderie of an all-male group whose heroes live apart from society. Through some natural process radios fail, airplanes become fog-bound, or the next stagecoach does not leave for a week. Initiation into the exclusive group involves ritual, which binds the group together, and the identity of group members is intimately bound up with the group.

Women can join the group only by undergoing its rituals. They are always a threat, and men are their prey. Their actions are always treated with suspicion.

The structure underlying Hawks' comic films is regression to childhood and savagery, or reversal of traditional sex roles, by which women dominate men, as in *I Was a Male War Bride* (1949).

In Hawks' films, then, the underlying dialectical structures are: the self-sufficient and the dominated; individual versus the wilderness; male versus female; accomplishment versus regression; insider versus outsider.

According to structuralists we will understand and appreciate a film once we penetrate to these deep structures. The alternative is to talk about the historical timing of a film, about its plots, its actors, its social message, and so on—matters that, according to structuralists, miss the dynamics of the film.

It has been a main objective of this book to indicate how an historical conception of film governs our appreciation of the medium. Many examples have been given that counter the structuralist theory, showing that the mean-ing and aesthetic qualities of shots, scenes, and even whole films depend on historical characteristics—the time in which the film was made or the time in which the film is experienced. In light of all these instances that run counter to the antihistorical thrust of structuralist theory, it would seem that the applica-bility to film of the structuralist approach is overstated.

While deep dialectical structures, such as those in the works of Hawks, are among the most crucial in appreciating films aesthetically, they are not the only factors. Its antihistorical bias aside, the structuralist approach offers another useful way of enriching our appreciation of films.

Because the comic film is a genre in which dialectic structures stand out clearly, examples from this genre are particularly useful in illustrating how these structures function. In the worlds of Charlie Chaplin and Buster Keaton, objects are as much protagonists as are the two clowns. Objects are endowed with almost human personalities. One thinks in this connection especially of the machinery in *Modern Times* and of that huge engine that Keaton rides in *The General* (1926).

Though there is a dialectical interaction between each of these comics and the objects, it takes different forms. In Chaplin's movies, objects are enemies to be overcome, though, as Bazin quite correctly points out, Charlie's method is more a process of getting around the situation than of working out a solution (such as defeating the object).[14] Keaton has a passion for the huge object: dinosaurs, waterfalls, an ocean liner, a train, entire armies, a steamboat, a

[14] Bazin, op. cit., p. 145.

storm at sea, and the New York police force.[15] In his films, the dialectic involving these objects is progressive with the huge object an antagonist at the beginning and an ally at the end.

The great engine starts of its own accord and, before he knows it, Buster is off and running, carried along by its power. It acts up: steam pours out of it, a fire breaks out, and it runs on inexorably. Buster is drenched, almost killed by a cannon towed by the engine, and nearly impaled on its cowcatcher. Gradually, however, the engine becomes Buster's faithful companion as he and it hold their own against the train robbers they are pursuing.

In this dialectical interaction with objects, each of the two comics has a distinct relation to nature. The Keaton character, in his many disguises, is dwarfed by the collosal works of nature around him. Keaton uses the long-take style and his favorite camera position is a long shot. Both emphasize his smallness in relation to objects. Chaplin also uses the long take, but prefers the close-in camera position, his comedy being of a much more intimate sort. This style is evident in *Gold Rush*. Though the great outdoors of the Yukon is the locale for this story, most of the action takes place in interiors—inside a little house, while an arctic storm rages outside, in a dance hall, or in Charlie's room in the Klondike town.

Other films also illustrate the use of dialectic. Milos Forman's *Taking Off* (1971) sets in motion a dialectic between the film's action and· the viewer's expectations that is a source of both humor and social commentary. *Taking Off* deals with the problems of contemporary life—runaway children, repressions, the vagaries of modern bureaucracy, and the like. The expectations of its initial audience were based mainly on the comedies of the golden era of comedy— the films of Mack Sennett, Chaplin, Keaton, Harold Lloyd, and the Marx Brothers. *Taking Off* undercut these expectations in a way that made the film an unsatisfying experience, an experience that corresponded to the theme of the film, throughout which pace, momentum, and excitement are built up and then cut short. In an unsatisfying chase sequence, Buck Henry, in his search for his runaway daughter, discovers someone else's runaway. He summons the runaway's mother who, in turn, begins her chase of *her* daughter. Pursuing the mother is a cab driver trying to get his fare, and Buck Henry in turn chases them. Finally, three tough "bikers," companions of the runaway, chase Henry. All of the ingredients are present for a typical madcap chase. The chase, however, is cut short (relative to what it would have been in the "golden era" comedies). In addition, a long lens is used, compressing the action and thus denying it the scope we would associate with such a scene.

A similarly unsatisfying scene concludes *Taking Off:* The runaway daughter has returned, bringing her hippie musician boyfriend. He is coaxed into singing one of his numbers, which the audience expects to be a contemporary

---

[15] Keaton's style is explored in Gerald Mast, *The Comic Mind* (New York: Bobbs-Merrill, 1973), pp. 125–148.

rock song. Instead, there is a cut to Buck Henry singing the outdated "Strangers in Paradise."

Taking Off leaves the audience feeling that no solutions have been worked out. The daughter may run away again; the parents may well continue to lead their repressed lives, and so on. Forman doesn't want to leave his audience with a feeling of satisfaction.

Jean Renoir builds his films upon a dialectical interaction between the rules governing the relationships of individuals and the spontaneity of nature and of man's natural responses. In Chapter 5, we saw how Renoir gave concrete visual form to this dialectic in *Boudu Saved from Drowning.* In *A Day in the Country* (1936) Parisians are contrasted to people who live close to nature. The former try to fulfill a felt obligation to commune with nature, an obligation they feel only one day a year. Their efforts turn out to be the fulfillment of a romanticized idea rather than any real contact with nature.

The country people, amused by their efforts, take advantage of them. In a charming image embodying the contrast between the urbanites and the country folk, we see the Parisians picnic in the outdoors, with all its annoyances, while the natives dine indoors.

The Rules of the Game (see page 134) is built upon a more complex structure of opposites. Main plots and subplots (involving the masters of a mansion and their guests and servants) set natural feelings of sexual attraction and love against the social conventions that govern their expression. The physical closeness of death, in a hunt scene where we see rabbits die in agonizing close-up, is set against the obscurity of death in the final scene, where we do not quite see a main character who was killed earlier. The surface gaiety of parties in the mansion is juxtaposed with the underlying coldness that marks the life of these people, who prefer not to live by the voice of spontaneity but rather by the rules of the game.

While not a comedy, Renoir's *The Grand Illusion* (1937) portrays in an interesting dialectical fashion the decline of the European aristocratic system and the rise of the new bourgeoise- and worker-dominated society. The setting is a prisoner-of-war camp during World War I. The action of the film brings out the decadence and artificiality of the ruling class and its mores and conventions. Such rules compel the German commander (Erich von Stroheim) to kill the man to whom he feels the closest, the French captain, a man of the commander's own social class. (The commanding officer must shoot escaping prisoners, while a prisoner who is a member of the social and military hierarchy is obligated to try to escape.) During the escape attempt in which the French captain is killed, two prisoners representative of the new order succeed in getting away. The men struggle to reach the Swiss border and the safety it promises. When they do, they find that there is nothing identifiable as such; snow covers everything. The invisibility of the border is a brilliant visual metaphor for the illusory nature of the social barriers that have formed so much of the dialectic of the film.

The Self-reflective Structure

Another prominent interpretive form, which may be called the "self-reflective structure," is applicable to films whose subject matter is the medium of film itself. This self-reflective structure is characteristic of modern art in general, which has often taken the curious form of reflections on art itself. Instead of using a given medium to create an art object that is to be appreciated by an audience, creative effort is bent upon bringing out the nature of the medium and making the audience aware of it.

Andy Warhol has been a leader in this trend in a wide variety of artistic media. His paintings, ready-mades, silkscreens, and films deal with the basic dimensions and structure of art media. His films of 1963 and 1964 are especially interesting in this connection. *Sleep, Kiss, Haircut,* and *Empire* explore the film medium through stationary camera recordings of minimal actions devoid of sound or story. These films may be viewed as tactics for inducing the audience to consider what they are doing when they seek to appreciate art.

Jean Luc-Godard has made calling attention to the film medium an element of his personal style. In his later films *(Wind From the East, Sympathy For the Devil, Tout Va Bien),* the viewer's attention is constantly drawn to the act of filming and to its implications for the experience that the audience is having.[16]

This artistic self-consciousness is found in film genres: Preston Sturges' comedy *Sullivan's Travels* (1941) has an opening sequence where a studio czar and a director debate the merits of making a film with a social message. Stanley Donen's *Singin' in the Rain* parodies the film-star system that it so obviously utilizes. John Cassavetes' *Minnie and Moscowitz* includes sequences from Bogart thrillers that disrupt the flow of action with the motive of calling attention to the medium.

Beckett's *Film*

Samuel Beckett's works also exemplify this form of creative expression. Through radio dramas, a TV production, several plays, novels, and his only motion picture, entitled *Film* (1964), Beckett seeks to turn the appreciator's consciousness upon the medium.[17] Those who experience his creations should not expect to be provided with either satisfaction or an opportunity to share another's fantasy.

In *Film,* the protagonist (O) attempts to achieve non-being by hiding from all vision. To do so, he removes or covers all sources of vision (divine, animal, human, even mechanical). Nevertheless, *esse est percipi* ("to be is to be perceived") prevails because there is no escape from self-perception, and all that remains is confrontation with the past as embodied in seven photographs.

[16] The best analysis of Godard's style during the later 1960s and early 1970s is Brian Henderson's "Toward a Non-Bourgeois Camera Style," *Film Quarterly,* Vol. 24, No. 2 (Winter 1970–71), pp. 2–14.
[17] It should be recognized that Alan Schneider, the director of *Film,* made an important contribution to its artistic character.

Though O destroys these, he can not destroy identity itself, for he is unavoidably perceived by the self, making of the dictum—to be is to be perceived—not only a metaphysical truth but also a formal limitation of the medium.

Film provides a kind of impressionistic sketch of the essential creative properties of the cinematic medium, which are regarded as primarily visual. To be sure, the film medium can be artistic by virtue of something artistic within it, such as dialogue (witness screen adaptations of Shakespeare), but cinematic art must work primarily through the visual. In *Film,* all that exists is captured by the vision of the camera in a portrayal of the medium that attempts to make us aware of it and of our relation to it. Though these two aspects are intimately bound up with one another, they can to some extent be considered separately.

Beckett's impression of film is that it is a series of stills with primarily visual content, constantly in motion, capable of portraying radical discontinuities of space and time, which provides an opportunity to escape the perception of actor, others, and oneself. His reflections on cinema start with the title, which may be viewed as an extended pun, for in describing the experience of *Film* one could as easily be describing the experience of film.

The film medium is, from one viewpoint, simply a series of stills. Beckett's *Film* contains such a series of stills, seen when Buster Keaton (O) peruses the seven still photographs that give glimpses of his earlier life, and that can also be regarded as a film within a film. These also display the capacity of the film medium to shift time and place—forward or backward—instantaneously, making for a highly flexible mode of expression.

Film also brings out the dialectics involved in the experience of watching a movie. Physically, there are certain affinities between our actions and those of O, who avoids the perception of others and himself. Through most of *Film,* E (the camera) views O from an angle that precludes direct perception of the latter's face. In the movie theatre, we all sit in darkness, facing in the same direction. So placed, we may be regarded as shunning the sight of others and ourselves. We speak sometimes of "escaping" into the world of the movie or of "losing ourselves" in a movie plot. We might as easily admit to a desire to share another's fantasy. In that darkened place where we watch movies, we are like O; we want that obscurity and isolation.

Motion, another essential feature of both *Film* and the film medium, is manifest in Keaton's almost constant movement in relation to the camera in the early scenes—on the street, the stairs to his room, and in his room. Viewing a movie, we constantly contend with motion. No sooner have we perceived a scene then it is changed. By contrast with the experience of viewing a painting, where we have the opportunity to contemplate and to abandon ourselves to our associations, movies interrupt our attempts at contemplation and association by providing a continuous flux. One feels: "I cannot think what I want to think. My thoughts must pursue moving objects."

There is a similar anguish in *Film.* Once O has taken all his measures to remove perception, he is at rest, leaving himself open to reflection upon himself. After he has destroyed the film within the film (by tearing up the photo sequence), he is in an arrested state that permits the self-confrontation that ends *Film*—when O discovers that E is himself (or his self perceiving himself).

Film exemplifies the primarily visual nature of the medium. The witty touch of a woman (in the scene in the street) saying "ssh" to her companion ensures that we recognize that the drama of O-E is played out on a landscape that happens to be silent but that could have sound. (She cautions against dialogue so that the distinctively cinematic may be sought.) *Film* explores what is distinctively cinematic—that is, the action of the camera, which provides us with vision not only of the greater world (the street) and the smaller world (the stairs and room) but also of the smallest, the inner world (the person, the self).

Film also exemplifies another essential feature of the cinematic medium— the peculiar nature of the film actor's audience (a mechanical contrivance) and his relation to it. As Pirandello wrote:

> The film actor feels as if in exile—exiled not only from the stage but also from himself. With a vague sense of discomfort he feels inexplicable emptiness: his body loses its corporeality, it evaporates, it is deprived of reality, life, voice, and the noises caused by moving about, in order to be changed into a mute image, flickering an instant on the screen, then vanishing into silence. . . . Then the projector will play with his shadow before the public, and he himself must be content to play before the camera.[18]

The feeling of strangeness that overcomes the actor before the camera, as Pirandello describes it, is basically the same as the estrangement felt before one's own image in the mirror. The ending of *Film* may exhibit this estrangement of the film actor from us. There is a barrier between O and us; we cannot see him and he cannot see us. The reality is that he once was somewhere where we were not, and now we are somewhere where he is not.

We have noted, with respect to O's examination of the stills, that this sequence may be regarded as a film within a film. The sequence also brings to consciousness in the audience the thought that they are watching a film—a recognition that is normally banished to the farthest corners of our minds.

The fact that it is the face of a well-known actor that is revealed to us in the final scene also reminds us that *Film* is only a film. To the extent that we are made aware of the medium, our traditional relation to it is shattered. Ordinarily, we experience art in a given medium by *passing over* the medium. Much as we use a window without seeing the window itself, so we look past the fact that we are only seeing a series of stills projected at the rate of twenty-four frames per second onto a screen. Once we are made to pause in our relation to the medium, we are removed from our role as spectators. Indeed much of modern art may be viewed as an evolutionary process leading to our removal from the role of spectators.

Beckett's *Film* is about our not knowing what film is about. Also, Beckett does what Keaton before him did—but in different ways. Where Keaton played

---

[18] From Luigi Pirandello's novel *Si Gira*.

all of us in his films—directly putting us in contact with ourselves—Beckett uses the indirect methods of reflection on the medium and use of tactics to make film into a form of self-knowledge.

Ambiguity and Knowing

Films that have ambiguous content bring to the fore the problem—the difficulty, and even the impossibility—of knowing the world. They offer perhaps the greatest challenge to the critic's interpretive abilities.

Cammell and Roeg's *Performance* (1970) is a version of the Hesse novel *Steppenwolf* updated to a contemporary London setting. Its Steppenwolf character has one foot in a gangster ring and the other in a drug subculture ruled by an ex-pop idol named Turner. There are numerous character changes, personality transformations, and exchanges of identity.

Performance has its source in Hesse's philosophy: Reality can be understood from multiple standpoints only; a kind of Jungian collective unconscious is required for knowledge; and identity is not unitary—rather, each of us *is* the roles he plays, the guises he assumes, the performances he gives.

In the course of *Performance,* the viewer witnesses a series of events whose intelligibility depends on their being taken as events seen from many points of view that are merged. Codirectors Donald Cammell and Nicolas Roeg seem to feel that grappling with the film's multiple viewpoint will sensitize the viewer to the complexities of reality.

Akira Kurosawa's *Rashomon* (1950) also deals with the problem of knowing the reality of a situation. Several versions of an event are presented, each revealing the individual teller's personal concern with pride. The problematic character of the situation arises primarily from a conflict in the accounts of the same event by the principals—a lord, his bride, a bandit, and a woodcutter. These accounts are reported by those who attended the trial. The lord (who speaks through a shaman) is reported to have said that his wife dishonored him, requiring him to commit an honorable suicide. The bandit is said to have recounted that he overpowered the husband, raped his wife before his eyes, and then defeated him in a duel of honor. The wife is reported to have told of being attacked, of being scorned by her husband because of it, of fainting, and of recovering her senses to find her husband dead. The woodcutter is alleged to have said that the bandit attacked the woman, then offered to fight her husband in order to win the right to marry her. The husband, who first refused to fight, was incited to do so by the anger of his wife and died in battle with the bandit.

To the complexity and the conflicts—as barriers to penetrating the truth of the incident—one must add the dazzling, impressionistic visual style and the distractingly engaging characters and their relationships.

Certain scenes in Marx Brothers films call into question certain audience expectations about what can happen in reality (even that of a film). In *A Night*

A Night at the Opera, *1935*

at the Opera (1935) dozens of people are crowded into a tiny stateroom that the viewer believes can only hold half that many. We cannot believe what we see, yet we see it. Just as the film as a whole makes us question the convention that people should be attentive and polite at the opera, so in this scene we question our assumptions about perception.

In *Duck Soup* (1933) Harpo seems to pull a gun, but we see that it is actually a feather duster. Just as we laugh, the duster turns into a revolver.

Perhaps the most intriguing of the films structured around the question "What is reality?" is Antonioni's *Blow-Up* (1967). The story centers around a photographer, Tom, who accidentally photographs what seems to be a homicide. He makes this discovery when he develops the photographs. A woman, shown by the photographs to have been embracing the victim before he was killed, desperately tries to obtain the pictures. Tom returns to the park where the photos were taken and finds a body. All but one extreme enlargement ("blow-up") of the dead man are stolen from Tom's studio. A friend remarks that it looks like one of her husband's abstract paintings—a fitting remark in the context of this film, since abstract art invites interpretation.

When Tom returns again to the murder scene, the body is gone. Walking back through the park, he encounters a group of people dressed as clowns who pretend to be players and spectators at a tennis game. They have no rackets or other equipment, and all of their activity is make-believe. When they pretend that one of their imaginary tennis balls has gone over the fence, Tom pretends to retrieve it, "throwing" the nonexistent ball back. As the "game" resumes, Tom hears the sound of the ball bouncing on the court. The film ends with Tom gone from the screen.

To appreciate the comment that the film makes at the end about our relationship to reality, we have to look back at key scenes in the film. In earlier scenes, offscreen presence has been strongly implied. In a scene in his studio where Tom flirts with some dippy girls, he ends by wrestling with them. A brief shot in the sequence reveals that a man is standing in the background. Viewers can be counted on not to see this presence because their attention is fixed on the wrestling match. A viewer who, on subsequent viewing of *Blow-Up,* notices the presence of the watching man is put into a position similar to Tom's—that of focusing on one part of a scene (in the park) while failing to notice something important (the murder) happening elsewhere.

Blow-Up, *1967*

Throughout *Blow-Up* the subjectivity of the camera is emphasized, and the importance of things is shown to depend on subjective factors (for example, the casualness with which Tom discards a guitar he had won earlier). When Tom hears the sounds of the nonexistent tennis game, he has begun to question the "truth" of the photographic image as well as the reality of what he has seen. In the closing scene, Antonioni dramatizes this uncertain relationship (of perceiver to reality) by eliminating Tom from the screen, leaving viewers divested of something they took to be most real in the world of this film. The point brought home is that Antonioni, in exercising his powers as a motion-picture maker, can create and take away things, as can a still photographer like Tom. The reality before either type of camera is a function of the will, the subjectivity, of the photographer and of the mysterious workings of that elusive thing we call "reality."

evaluating films

A third level of critical activity (pages 137, 153), that of determining the aesthetic qualities of a film, depends upon the other two—description and interpretation. For example, a film has the aesthetic quality of unity if its visual elements, sound, and affects fit together in a coherent fashion or an overall interpretive pattern structures them into a whole. Numerous examples have been provided throughout this book on how judgments of aesthetic qualities have this dependency on description and interpretation. The humor of Chaplin, the tension of the Hitchcock film, the unity of *Citizen Kane,* the beauty of the fogs in *The Informer,* the intensity of *Breathless,* the black humor of *Dr. Strangelove,* the zaniness of the Marx Brothers, the complexity of *Last Year At Marienbad,* the moving quality of *Nosferatu,* and the poignancy of *La Strada* have all been shown to be aesthetic qualities dependent on first- and second-level characteristics.

The critic's act of passing judgment on a film (the fourth level of criticism) involves deciding that the film is an artistic success or failure. Such judgments are made by reference to the film's aesthetic qualities; hence the dependency on third-level criticism.

For example, when film comedies are good or bad aesthetically, their success or failure is traceable in part to the extent they possess the quality of being funny. Evaluations of success or failure in film can be seen, then, to be evaluations of whether the film is good or bad of a kind or kinds. If we decide that Chaplin's *The Gold Rush* is good, this statement is an elliptical way of saying that it is a good film *of this kind.* Its "kind" is a complex matter; as noted above, it includes being a comedy.

The features of a film are identified at the descriptive and interpretive levels. Some are obvious, like the fact that *The Gold Rush* is a comedy. Others are more subtle, involving creative interpretation on the part of the critic or appreciator. Structuralists would point to the dialectic structures that run through *The Gold Rush.* The film is structured around oppositions, including the individual versus untamed nature, warmth versus cold, the outer versus the inner life, and the material versus the spiritual side of human nature. An assessment of the artistic success of the film is made partly in terms of whether these structural features mold *The Gold Rush* into a unified whole.

For a film like *The Gold Rush,* being funny and being unified count toward a favorable verdict. These aesthetic qualities are valuable in this film because of the kind of film it is. In other films, most notably in films such as those of Godard and Warhol, it is often true that disunity counts toward a judgment that the work is a success. The descriptive and interpretive discussion of dislocation in Chapter 4 showed how structures of disunity in space, time, and action can be used with artistic intent.

It follows from the dependency of the process of evaluation on description and interpretation that there are, on the whole, no general rules governing the making of judgments about films. General features do not count toward a favorable verdict. Being funny, being tragic, being unified, cannot be said to make a film good. The features that *can* count depend on the kind of artistic entity the film is identified to be on the descriptive and interpretive levels. Once having isolated the cluster of "kinds" that the film is, the critic can set about judging how successfully the film has fulfilled the things those kinds of film demand. If it is a comedy, how funny is it? If a film that presents a tightly knit story, how unified is the final outcome? If a film with a dislocating structure, does it leave the audience productively disposed (in the Brechtian sense) or merely confused and dissatisfied.

Criteria of Aesthetic Value

The Quality of Being "Cinematic"

It has often been supposed that being "cinematic" is another feature that counts toward a favorable verdict on a film.[1] That is, if a film tells its story, develops its characters, communicates its social message, or creates its aesthetic qualities primarily in terms of aspects unique to the medium, then the film rates a highly favorable verdict. Putting it another way, one might say that the film is better aesthetically than some counterpart would be that creates its aesthetic effects by relying on features not unique to the medium. This view is usually based on the belief that a film should do what only film can, rather than what theatre or literature or some other medium can. Otherwise, why make a film rather than stage a play or write a novel? In line with this concept, a film fails to be cinematic if it creates its aesthetic qualities, tells its story, and develops its characters by relying primarily on such things as dialogue or offscreen narration or theatrical *mise en scène*. Correlatively, being cinematic involves such things as revealing character and situation visually and through sound quality rather than via dialogue and creating *mise en scène* primarily by camera movement, shooting angle, and editing rather than simply by make-up, costume, and sets.

Supporters of this notion believe that a film will fail unless it utilizes cinematic devices in its shaping. A film that uses a static camera, for example, can give a diminished sense of three-dimensionality and be lifeless and uninteresting. In the theatre, viewers have real people and real objects before them. No effort has to be made to give them plastic qualities. In film, however, the materials that the viewer relates to are, in effect, large shadows—patterns of light and shade on a screen. Effort must be expended to give them a semblance of life.

It may be acknowledged that, if a film is to involve an audience, cinematic features must be utilized in it. If a film is merely a filmed play, with a more or less static camera, with the *mise en scène* no more than what would exist in the theatre, and with every event explained by dialogue and offscreen narration, the film will more than likely be an artistic failure. It does not follow, however, that the features that make a particular scene or whole film good have to be cinematic features.

Franco Zefferelli's film adaptation of Shakespeare's *Romeo and Juliet* (1968) utilized the lines of the play in creating aesthetic qualities in the film. At the same time, a necessary condition for artistic success in film was satisfied. Staging of many scenes drew upon the full resources of the cinematic medium

---

[1] For an illuminating discussion of the idea of being "cinematic," see Susan Sontag, "Film and Theatre," in Gerald Mast and Marshall Cohen, eds., *Film Theory and Criticism* (New York: Oxford University Press, 1974), pp. 249–67.

to give a vivid sense of three-dimensionality, liveliness, and motion—in short, the illusion of a real-life scene. But it cannot be said that the success of the film was to be traced primarily to these cinematic effects: The feature that contributed as much as any to the aesthetic quality was the superb poetry of the Shakespearean drama.

Indeed, if *Romeo and Juliet* were to be made in a way that sacrificed its dialogue in order to emphasize the cinematic, would we not have something of less aesthetic value than Zefferelli's version? To say that we know, before we experience a film, that being cinematic is always preferable to using one of these features—a piece of dialogue, theatrical *mise en scène,* or offscreen narration—is to overlook the importance of context. Though filmmakers may well be encouraged to explore the cinematic features of film rather than those held in common with other media, it is not necessarily true that every film in which cinematic features predominate will be better.

Being a Mass Medium

Another criterion of aesthetic value arises from a conception of the cinematic medium as a *mass* medium. It is supposed that, as a popular art, film must appeal to a mass audience.

The example of film comedy is often cited in this connection. To appreciate fully films in this genre, the moviegoer should watch them in the company of a large audience. Much of the humor one finds in comedy results from the triggering of one's responses by the laughter of the rest of the audience. Supporters of this view point to how the experience of watching comic films on television or in a relatively empty movie theatre differs from watching them in a crowded theatre.

The claim concerning mass appeal is not, of course, restricted to film comedy. Some aspects of the excitement of adventure dramas, the tension of suspense stories, and the moving quality of love stories are traceable to the experience of watching the movie in a mass situation.

In order to assess this claim concerning mass appeal, an understanding is needed of what a "mass" is. Denis McQuail has provided a useful summary of thinking on this topic.[2] His first observation is that no definition of the term is fully satisfactory. Instead, it is more useful to think of "massness" as a continuum.[3] This is so because "most if not all of the [massness-making] characteristics will be present in varying degrees in a mass communication situation. . . ."[4]

What are the "massness-making" characteristics? Mass media are directed at large audiences—larger than audiences of other forms of communication

[2] Denis McQuail, *Toward A Sociology of Mass Communication* (London: Collier-MacMillan, 1969), Chapter 1, pp. 1–17.
[3] Ibid., p. 10.
[4] Ibid.

(for example, a lecture). Mass communications are public, the content open to all and the distribution relatively unstructured and informal. The audience for mass communications is heterogeneous; it includes people living under widely different conditions, people from different cultures and positions in society, people engaged in widely differing occupations, and, hence, people having differing interests and standards of living. The channel of mass communication is one-way in nature: The communicator is impersonal; the audience is anonymous. Public opinion polls and correspondence provide some feedback, but ordinarily the mass communicator conveys material without any response from the audience.

Mass audiences are groups united by a simultaneous interest. Members of the group are not, however, known to one another and have the most restricted kinds of interaction. Reactions are relatively uniform, though membership in the group is constantly changing. No leadership or feelings of identity unite the group, which is quite loosely organized. The channel of communication to which the group relates, however, is organized in quite a complex and formal way, with well-defined systems of production and distribution.

A television program on the national elections would most likely fall at that end of the continuum where massness is maximal (call it "high mass"). At an intermediate position on the continuum might be the report of a crime in a big city newspaper. The receivers of this communication would form a smaller group, selecting the piece of communication according to their interests, occupations, and the like. Reactions could differ rather markedly, and contact of the medium with the receivers would not be simultaneous. At the "low mass" end of the continuum would be the reading of an item in a local newspaper, for which the audience would be small, more homogeneous, with anonymity markedly low, communicators probably known personally, and feedback common.

The production, distribution, and exhibition of films has dictated that, by and large, film's audience be a mass audience. The enormous costs involved in each of these activities of the film industry have motivated filmmakers, producers, and others involved to make creative decisions in terms of capturing the mass audience that is needed to finance the industry; hence films have been built on themes that tend toward the universal. Mythic and glamorized characters have frequently dominated; sensational subject matter, such as sex and violence, have been exploited; and issues have been portrayed in a relatively simplistic fashion. There is, however, nothing intrinsic to the essential features of the medium that makes film a mass medium. Were circumstances to change, so that it became financially unnecessary to reach a large number of people, there would be no reason why films could not be made for nonmass audiences.

McQuail supports the view that there is nothing essential to the medium of film that requires that it always be a mass medium. To date, most films have been designed to affect an audience which is, by the nature of the prevailing method of exhibition, a mass audience. To fail to take this mass feature of the audience into account is to overlook something important, both about a film's intent and its effect.

It is important to recognize that this status for film carries no negative implications. How a mass medium is used determines whether it will have positive or negative consequences for society. Many commentators, however, view mass media as contributing to many societal ills: alienation; reduction of culture to the lowest level (with crucial societal decisions being made on irrational grounds); and increased violence and apathy.

Reaching the widest audience involves appealing to the lowest common denominator, which, in turn, involves pandering to prurient interests, the desire to witness violence, tendencies to stereotype and simplify, sentimentality, and the desire for escapist entertainment.

There are many ways (apart from appealing to the lowest common denominator) in which a film, its distribution, and exhibition can be structured so as to achieve a high degree of mass appeal. One need only consider Chaplin's comedy to recognize the deficiencies of this pejorative image of the mass media. A film like *Modern Times* (which relies upon myths and universal themes) is well attuned to a mass audience yet touches some of our highest emotions and provides useful ideas about society.

Semiology

Much thought about the film medium and film criticism (especially structuralism) has been devoted to development of a so-called *semiology* of the cinema. Semiology is the study (or logic) of signs. A semiological investigation of cinema would attempt to reduce film criticism and theory to a study of film as a system of signs, which would tend to make it almost a branch of linguistics.

According to semiological theory, the film critic and film theorist should treat film as a language, their task being to ferret out a film grammar—that is, the laws governing the way a filmmaker communicates via cinematic signs. All phases of film criticism would thereby be made more rigorous and more scientific.

Peter Wollen justifies subsuming film criticism under a general scientific study of the systems of signs as follows:

> . . . Semiology is a vital area of study for the aesthetics of film. . . . Any criticism necessarily depends upon knowing what a text means, being able to read it. Unless we understand the code or mode of expression which permits meaning to exist in the cinema, we are condemned to massive imprecision and nebulosity in film criticism, an unfounded reliance on intuition and momentary impressions."[5]

---

[5] Peter Wollen, *Signs and Meaning in the Cinema* (Bloomington: University of Indiana Press, 1969), pp. 16–17.

With film grammar at our disposal, we can decipher the meaning of "film texts." To interpret a film, therefore, is to recognize how its visual and aural elements function as signs. The semiological approach would also be used to determine a film's aesthetic qualities and to evaluate films.

Instead of being the subjective and momentary impressions of the critic, then, aesthetic judgments and verdicts on films would become an outgrowth of scientific investigation. For example, disagreements about whether a Hawks film is unified or moving or funny and whether it is aesthetically good can be resolved by reference to the way it communicates with an audience via a system of signs that form a language, a film language. Thus, one who knows film language could objectively settle questions about what a film communicates and whether it does so in an artistically successful way.

The analysis of description and interpretation earlier in this section provides reasons for questioning some of the assumptions made by those who would have a semiology of cinema. As established above, structuralists have not discovered superior ways to describe and interpret films. With their antihistorical emphasis an essential feature of the medium is left out. At best they provide only one of many equally acceptable modes of interpretation. It is also true that if semiology is to make a contribution to our understanding of the medium and to film criticism, it will have to do so in conjunction with other approaches. To base description, interpretation, aesthetic judgment, and evaluation of films on a general theory of signs alone would be too restrictive.

Furthermore, there are reasons for questioning whether a semiology of cinema is even possible. The extremely specific ways in which a film's visual, aural, and affective qualities make it aesthetically good or bad pose a problem that may be semiologically insurmountable. When the film critic seeks to evaluate a scene in a motion picture, he must deal with the fact that *every quality* of the scene may be influential. This is a situation with which a scientist does not have to contend. For example, in determining whether a speech act is grammatical, a linguist need take into account only certain features of the sounds the speaker makes. By contrast, in evaluating a scene, the film critic must take into consideration *all* features of the sounds the performers make in speaking (as we saw in Chapter 2). Thus, in formulating generalizations about which features of a scene make it work aesthetically, the film critic finds himself overwhelmed with possibilities.

Perhaps the film critic should acknowledge that he is in a situation different from the linguist's, and that he is unable to be "scientific" about his evaluations. The film critic works with more qualities than he has (or would want to have) names for. It also seems likely that one can grasp the features that make films good or bad without having names or generalizations for them.

As noted above, we know that the fact that *Citizen Kane* has unity (by virtue of its visual and sound editing) contributes to its artistic success. We also know that visual *dis*unity contributes to the success of *Breathless*. We *know* these connections between the presence of aesthetic qualities and judgments, though no one can formulate a generalization that would fulfill the standards of scientific inquiry and explain why these connections hold.

In summary, film criticism is an art and relies on nonscientific modes of understanding. An aesthetician has observed:

> Is it reasonable to expect better evaluations of art after a thousand years of criticism that before? . . . I do think that some critical judgments have been and are every day being "proved" as well as, in the nature of the case, they ever can be proved.[6]

Accepting this outlook would not imply that the general theory of signs has no value for film theory or criticism. Semiology, like other social sciences, provides ideas and connections that enrich our understanding and sharpen our perceptions. What is excluded, however, is the notion that the film critic should become—above all other things—a theorist in a special branch of the theory of signs. The nature of the material critics deal with requires instead that they excel in a form of creative activity. Criticism must be a synthesis based on knowledge gained from many sources (including linguistics). In fact, film critics can be as creative as the artists whose work they study.

[6] Arnold Isenberg, "Critical Communication," in Francis J. Coleman, *Contemporary Studies in Aesthetics* (New York: McGraw-Hill, 1968), p. 149.

Plate I Elvira Madigan, *1967*

Plate II   Two for the Road, *1966*

Plate III   Fellini's Satyricon, *1969*

Plate IV   Fellini's Satyricon, *1969*

Plate V   Bonnie and Clyde, *1967*

Plate VI   Blow-Up, *1967*

Plate VII   Cabaret, *1972*

appendix

bibliography/filmography

Chapter 1

The perception of visual qualities in art
Arnheim, Rudolf. *Art and Visual Perception.* Berkeley: University of California Press, 1969.

Gibson, James J. *The Perception of the Visual World.* Boston: Houghton Mifflin, 1950.

Gombrich, Ernst Hans Josef. *Meditations on a Hobby Horse and Other Essays on the Theory of Art.* London: Phaidon Publishers, 1963.

Kepes, Gyorgy. *Language of Vision.* Chicago: P. Theobold, 1944.

Koffka, Kurt. *Principles of Gestalt Psychology.* New York: Harcourt Brace Jovanovich, 1935.

The visual aspects of film
Belazs, Bela. *Theory of the Film.* Translated by Edith Bone. New York: Dover, 1970. Contains the best discussion of the artistic uses of the close-up (pp. 60–88).

Bobker, Lee. *Elements of Film.* 2d ed. New York: Harcourt Brace Jovanovich, 1974. Includes well-chosen illustrations of the characteristic appearance produced by various lenses (pp. 72–78).

Cocteau, Jean. *Cocteau on the Film.* Translated by Vera Traill. New York: Dover, 1972. Includes valuable remarks on *mise en scène.*

Malkowicz, J. Kris. *Cinematography.* New York: Van Nostrand Reinhold Co., 1973. Has an especially useful discussion of filters, lenses, lighting, and optics.

Nilsen, Vladimir. *The Cinema as a Graphic Art.* New York: Hill and Wang, 1959. Has a particularly interesting treatment of camera position and shooting angle (pp. 31–48).

Panofsky, Erwin. "Style and Medium in the Motion Picture." *Critique,* no. 3 (1947).

Pincus, Edward. *Guide to Filmmaking.* New York: Signet, 1969. Treats technical aspects of filmmaking.

Pudovkin, V. I. *Film Technique and Film Acting.* Translated by Ivor Montagu. New York: Grove Press, 1970. Noteworthy discussion of editing and acting.

FILMS

Color emphasizes theme
> Antonioni, Michelangelo, *Red Desert* (1964)
> Demi, Jacques, *Umbrellas of Cherbourg* (1964)
> Donen, Stanley, *Funny Face* (1956)
> Kinugasa, Teinosuke, *Gate of Hell* (1953)

Mixture of color and black and white
> Fleming, Victor, *Wizard of Oz* (1939)
> Lelouch, Claude, *A Man and a Woman* (1966)
> Lewin, Albert, *Picture of Dorian Grey* (1945)
> Tati, Jacques, *Jour de Fête* (1947)

Negative color
> Lucas, George and Milius, John, *Marcello I'm So Bored* (1967)   A University of Southern California student film.

Onscreen space
> Clarke, Shirley, *The Connection* (1962)   Portrays action in a confined space with stationary and moving camera.
> Griffith, D. W., *Intolerance* (1914)   Utilizes a variety of alternatives to standard rectangular framing.
> Thompson, J. Lee, *Guns of Navarone* (1961)   Uses framing to create relationships of scale essential to the storyline.

Offscreen space
> Boorman, John, *Deliverance* (1972)
> Laughton, Charles, *Night of the Hunter* (1955)
> Polanski, Roman, *Repulsion* (1965)

Editing
> Eisenstein, Sergei, *Ivan the Terrible, Parts 1 and 2* (1943–46)

Mise en scène
> Hathaway, Henry, *Call Northside 777* (1948)   Exemplifies the *film noir* setting and lighting of the late 1940s and early 1950s in America.
> Reed, Sir Carol, *Odd Man Out* (1947)

Chapter 2

> Burch, Noel. *The Theory of Film Practice.* New York: Praeger, 1973. Pinpoints some of the most creative uses of sound in the films of Mizoguchi, Bresson, and Resnais (pp. 90–100).
> Eisenstein, Sergei. *The Film Sense.* New York: Meridian, 1942. Contains far-reaching analysis of the editing-together of visuals and music in the "Battle on the Ice" sequence from *Alexander Nevsky* (1938) (pp 175–216 and 282 facing page).
> Huntley, John, and Manvill, Roger. *The Technique of Film Music.* New York: Hastings House, 1959. Traces the use of music in film.
> Meyer, Leonard. *Music, the Arts and Ideas.* Chicago: University of Chicago Press, 1973. Includes description of twentieth-century music helpful in assessing integration of "nonfunctional" music in film.

FILMS

Dialogue
> Glenville, Peter, *Beckett* (1964)   Notable for its balance of dialogue with visual-auditory qualities.

Offscreen narration
> Truffaut, François, *Jules and Jim* (1962)

Natural sound
> Altman, Robert, *M*A*S*H* (1970), *McCabe and Mrs. Miller* (1971), *Thieves Like Us* (1974), and *Nashville* (1975)   Sacrifices clarity of dialogue for heightened sense of how people relate in everyday spaces.

Silence
> Bergman, Ingmar, *The Silence* (1964)   The absences of sound help express existential themes.

Chapter 3

Affect
> Beardsley, Monroe. *Aesthetics: Problems in the Philosophy of Criticism.* New York: Harcourt Brace Jovanovich, 1958. Chapter 1 contains a sustained argument that capacities to affect an audience are *not* part of a work of art.
> Dewey, John. *Art as Experience.* New York: G. P. Putnam and Sons, 1934. Considers the importance of taking affect into account in appreciating art objects.

Space in works of art
> Arnheim, Rudolf. *Art and Visual Perception.* Berkeley: University of California Press, 1969. Chapter 5 uses psychological investigations into appreciator response to art as grounds for analyzing the spatial aspect of visual art objects.
> Hauser, Arnold. *The Social History of Art,* vol. 2. New York: Vintage Books, 1963. Discusses Baroque artists' utilization of space in painting and sculpture (pp. 172–82).
> Rasmussen, Steen. *Experiencing Architecture.* Cambridge: MIT Press, 1959. Outlines the basic concepts for appreciating how architectural space is created.
> Read, Sir Herbert Edward. *The Art of Sculpture.* New York: Pantheon Books, 1956. Discusses the peculiarities of sculptural space.

Time in works of art
> Arnheim, Rudolf. *Art and Visual Perception.* Berkeley: University of California Press, 1969. Chapter 8 compares and contrasts time in a variety of visual art forms (pp. 360–68).
> Kinder, Marsha and Houston, Beverle. *Close-Up: A Critical Perspective on Film.* New York: Harcourt Brace Jovanovich, 1972. Includes an analysis of time in Cammel and Roeg's *Performance* (1970) (pp. 359–76).
> Meyerhoff, Hans. *Time in Literature.* Berkeley: University of California Press, 1955. Applies temporal concepts developed in science to literary works with implications for the understanding of time in art.
> Priestley, J. B. *Man and Time.* New York: Dell, 1964. An excellent summary of ideas about time and their application to art.
> Ward, John. *Alain Resnais or the Theme of Time.* Garden City, N.Y.: Doubleday and Co., 1968. Explores temporal concepts, including the classic treatment of time developed in Henri Bergson's *Time and Free Will* (London: Allen and Unwin, 1921).

FILMS

Spatial affect
> Canadian Film Board, *Corral* (1954)
> Weiss, Peter, *Marat Sade* (1967)   Produces a sense of a confinement through use of the camera.

Temporal affect
> Bresson, Robert, *Diary of a Country Priest* (1950), *A Man Condemned to Escape* (1956), and *Pickpocket* (1959)   With *The Trial of Joan of Arc* (1961)—discussed in

Chapter 8 of this text—these exemplify some of the most complex and aesthetically rewarding patterns of time in film.

Capra, Frank, *It's a Wonderful Life* (1946)   Noteworthy for juxtaposition of events.

Murnau, F. W., *Sunrise* (1927)   Noteworthy for juxtaposition of events.

Ray, Satyajit, *Pather Panchali* (1955)

Resnais, Alain, *All the Memories of the World* (1956)   Shows how the French Bibliotheque Nationale is the memory of mankind.

Resnais, Alain, *La Guerre est Finie* (1964), *Je t'aime, Je t'aime* (1969)   Explore futurity.

Chapter 4

Cavell, Stanley. *Must We Mean What We Say? A Book of Essays.* New York: Scribner, 1969. The essay on Beckett's *Endgame* provides a searching analysis of the role of expectation in experiencing modern art.

———. *The World Viewed: Reflections on the Ontology of Film.* New York: Viking Press, 1971. Chapter 5 provides insights on the relation of audience belief to the perception of film.

Egri, Lajos. *The Art of Dramatic Writing.* New York: Simon and Schuster, 1946. Explains the central role of conflict, and argues for the aesthetic necessity of conflict resolution in storyline films.

Gombrich, Ernst Hans Josef. *Art and Illusion; A Study on the Psychology of Pictorial Representation.* New York: Pantheon Books, 1960. Provides the most complete discussion of the role of perceptual illusion in art.

Hauser, Arnold. *The Social History of Art,* vol. 4. New York: Vintage Books, 1963. Discusses the historical dimension of the experience of art. See the section "The Film Age."

Jarvie, I. C. *Movies and Society.* New York: Basic Books, 1970. Contains valuable information on audience analysis.

Lipton, Lenny. *Independent Filmmaking.* San Francisco: Straight Arrow Books, 1972.

McLuhan, Marshall. *Understanding Media.* New York: Signet, 1964. Contains much stimulating material on audience reactions to media such as film.

Renan, Sheldon. *An Introduction to the American Underground Film.* New York: E. P. Dutton and Co., 1967.

Seldes, Gilbert. *The Great Audience.* New York: Viking Press, 1951.

FILMS

Antonioni, Michelangelo, *The Passenger* (1975)   An open thematic structure departs markedly from audience expectations.

Brakhage, Stan, *Cat's Cradle* (1958), *Blue Moses* (1962), *Dog Star Man* (1959–64), and *Sexual Meditations* (1973)   Challenges audience perceptual and emotional capacities to respond; more extreme than Godard's films.

Richardson, Tony, *Mademoiselle* (1966)   Total victory of evil over good violates standard audience expectations.

Chapter 5

Armes, Roy. *Film and Reality.* London: Penguin, 1974. Presents a historical survey of issues in film reality.

Balazs, Bela. *Theory of the Film.* New York: Dover, 1970. Note particularly Chapters 6–8.

Grierson, John. *Grierson on Documentary*. rev. ed. Edited and compiled by Forsyth Hardy. Berkeley: University of California Press, 1966. Deals with the question of whether documentaries portray reality.

Hegel, G. W. F. *Reason in History*. Translated by R. S. Hartman. New York: Library of Liberal Arts, 1953. Discusses the ideology underlying the dialectical concepts central to Eisenstein's approach.

Heller, Eric. *Artist's Journey into the Interior and Other Essays*. New York: Vintage Books, 1968. Chapter 4 provides a comprehensive discussion of the concept of being "realist."

Mamber, Stephen. *Cinema Vérité in America: Studies in Uncontrolled Documentary*. Cambridge: MIT Press, 1973.

Marx, Karl. *Capital, the Communist Manifesto and Other Writings by Karl Marx*. Edited by Max Eastman. New York: Modern Library, 1932. Like Hegel work cited above, this is important for understanding ideology underlying dialectical concepts.

Rotha, Paul. *Documentary Film*. London: Faber and Faber, 1958.

Weiss, Paul. *Cinematics*. Carbondale and Edwardsville: Southern Illinois Press, 1975. Philosophically difficult, this contains sometimes rewarding discussion of cinematic reality.

FILMS

Documentaries for assessing the portrayal of the real

Flaherty, Robert, *Moana* (1926) and *Man of Aran* (1934)

Lorentz, Pare, *The River* (1937)

Rouch, Jean, *Chronicle of a Summer* (1961)   Done in *cinema vérité;* with Edgar Morin.

Wiseman, Fred, *High School* (1967)

Neorealist films

Rossellini, Roberto, *Open City* (1945)

Visconti, Luchino, *La Terra Trema* (1948)

Other films of interest in terms of reality

Cassavetes, John, *Husbands* (1972) and *A Woman Under the Influence* (1974)

Donskoi, Mark, *The Childhood of Maxim Gorky* (1938), *My Apprenticeship* (1939), and *My Universities* (1940)

Chapter 6

Burch, Noel. *Theory of Film Practice*. New York: Praeger, 1973. Chapter 7 provides a most interesting discussion of chance in film.

Frye, Northrop. *Anatomy of Criticism*. Princeton: Princeton University Press, 1957. Explains the concept of the world of the work of art.

Malraux, André. "Art, Popular Art and the Illusion of the Folk." Translated by William Barrett. *Partisan Review*, no. 5 (1951). Develops ideas helpful for an appreciation of unreality in film expression.

Tyler, Parker. *Magic and Myth in the Movies*. New York: Simon and Schuster, 1970. Contains material relevant for identifying the aesthetic uses of the real and the unreal within the world of the film.

Young, Vernon. *Cinema Borealis: Ingmar Bergman and the Swedish Ethos*. New York: Avon, 1971. Helpful for understanding the world of Bergman films.

FILMS

Unreality within the world of the work

Bergman, Ingmar, *Sawdust and Tinsel* (1953)   The look and feel of unreality in its

opening sequence heightens the nightmare-like experience portrayed in the film.
Mann, Daniel, *Our Man Flint* (1966)   A *tour de force* of the unreal in the world of the
film.

Chance in the world of the work

Chabrol, Claude, *This Man Must Die* (1971)   Makes believeable the most absurdly
improbable events.

Chapter 7

Analysis of the surrealist style

Breton, André. *Manifestes du surrealisme.* Paris: Gallimard, 1963.
Brunius, Jacques. "Experimental Film in France." In Manvell, Roger, ed. *Experiment
in the Film.* London: Grey Walls Press, 1949.
Durgnat, Raymond. *Luis Buñuel.* Berkeley: University of California Press, 1968.
Matthews, J. H. *Surrealism and Film.* Ann Arbor: University of Michigan Press, 1971.
Taylor, John Russell. *Cinema Eye, Cinema Ear.* New York: Hill and Wang, 1964. The
chapter on Buñuel is particularly relevant.

FILMS

Brunius, Jacques, *Violins d'Ingres* (1939)
Coppola, Francis Ford, *The Conversation* (1973)
Deren, Maya, *Meshes in the Afternoon* (1943)
Rafelson, Bob, *King of Marvin Gardens* (1971)
Richter, Hans, *Dreams That Money Can Buy* (1944)
Sjoberg, Alf, *Miss Julie* (1950)

Chapter 8

Berenson, Bernard. *Aesthetics and History.* Garden City, N.Y.: Doubleday and Co.,
1948. Describes realist and other styles.
Knight, Arthur. *The Liveliest Art.* New York: New American Library, 1957. Contains a
wealth of material on the development of cinematic styles.
Richie, Donald. *Japanese Cinema: Film Style and National Character.* Garden City,
N.Y.: Doubleday and Co., 1961. Uses the Japanese experience to explore question
of comparative national cinematic styles.
Robbe-Grillet, Alain. *For a New Novel.* New York: Grove Press, 1965. Sheds light on
Robbe-Grillet's style as embodied in his script for the film *Last Year at Marienbad*
(1961).
Willett, John. *Expressionism.* New York: McGraw-Hill, 1970. Sets the historical
contexts from which this rich artistic movement arose.

FILMS

Realist: impressionistic

Ozu, Yasujiro, *Tokyo Story* (1953)
Seta, Vittorio de, *The Bandits of Orgosolo* (1961)
Tati, Jacques, *Mon Oncle* (1958)

Realist: naturalistic

Brooks, Richard, *Blackboard Jungle* (1956)

Peckinpah, Sam, *Straw Dogs* (1972)   Pushes the limits of naturalistic portrayal of violent subject matter.

Penn, Arthur, *Little Big Man* (1971)   Exemplifies, in its complex portrayal of the Indian figure, the 1970s vision of the American West.

Expressionist

Browning, Todd, *Freaks* (1932)

Hoffmann, Kurt, *Aren't We Wonderful* (1959)   A Greek chorus provides the expressionistic texture.

Lang, Fritz, *M* (1931)

Vigo, Jean, *Zero for Conduct* (1933)   Slow motion and bizarre touches give the action an expressionistic cast.

Wadja, Andrzej, *Ashes and Diamonds* (1959). Uses expressionistic imagery and an expressionistic telescoping of time.

Chapter 9

Battcock, Gregory. *The New Art.* New York: E. P. Dutton and Co., 1973. Explains how to relate to contemporary art.

Berlyne, D. E. *Aesthetics and Psychobiology.* New York: Appleton-Century-Crofts, 1971. Discusses the relevance of psychological investigations to the understanding of works of art.

Hirsch, E. E. *Validity in Interpretation.* New Haven: Yale University Press, 1967.

Kaufmann, Stanley. *A World on Film.* New York: Harper and Row, 1966. The section on *Red Desert* (1964) gives the best critical analysis of Antonioni's style.

Richie, Donald. *The Films of Akira Kurosawa.* Berkeley: University of California Press, 1965. Is the best source for interpretation of Kurosawa's films.

Myth and related topics

Campbell, Joseph. *The Hero with a Thousand Faces.* 3d ed. Princeton: Princeton University Press, 1973.

Miranda, Pierre, ed. *Mythology: Selected Readings.* Baltimore: Penguin, 1972.

Structuralism

Ehrmann, Jacques, ed. *Structuralism.* Garden City, N.Y.: Doubleday and Co., 1970.

Lane, Michael. *Introduction to Structuralism.* New York: Basic Books, 1970.

Robey, David, ed. *Structuralism: An Introduction.* Oxford: Oxford University Press, 1973.

Scholes, Robert. *Structuralism in Literature.* New Haven: Yale University Press, 1974.

FILMS

Myth

Camus, Marcel, *Black Orpheus* (1960)   Sets the Orpheus myth in Rio de Janeiro during Mardi Gras.

Teshigahara, Hiroshi, *Woman in the Dunes* (1964)

Ambiguity

Bergman, Ingmar, *The Silence* (1964)

Chabrol, Claude, *Les Bonnes Femmes* (1960), *Les Biches* (1968), and *Une Femme Infidel* (1969)   Contain characteristically ambiguous endings.

Clayton, Jack, *The Pumpkin Eater* (1964)

Preminger, Otto, *Anatomy of a Murder* (1959)   Structured so that no one interpretation can prove altogether satisfactory.

Ritt, Martin, *The Outrage* (1964)   An American adaptation of Kurosawa's *Rashomon* (1951). Useful in comparison with the Japanese film.

Chapter 10

Eco, Umberto. *A Theory of Semiotics.* Advances in Semiotics Series. Bloomington: University of Indiana Press, 1976.

Hume, David. *On the Standard of Taste.* New York: Bobbs-Merrill Co., 1957. Classic treatment of evaluation with a subjectivist approach.

Kaplan, Abraham. "The Aesthetics of the Popular Arts." *Journal of Aesthetics and Art Criticism,* no. 3 (1966), pp. 351–64.

Metz, Christian. *Film language: A Semiology of the Cinema.* Translated by Michael Taylor. Oxford: Oxford University Press, 1974.

Rosenberg, Jacob. *On Quality in Art, Criteria of Excellence, Past and Present.* Princeton: Princeton University Press, 1964. Provides a methodology for approaching objectivity in evaluation.

film sources

Andy Warhol (Factory Films)
33 Union Square W
New York NY 10003

Art Cinema Booking Service
1501 Broadway
New York NY 10036

Avco Embassy Pictures
1301 Ave. of the Americas
New York NY 10019

Blackhawk Films
Eastin-Phelan Corp.
Davenport IA 52808

Broadcasting and Film Commission
National Council of Churches
475 Riverside Dr.
New York NY 10027

Brunswick Film Library
200 S. Chester St.
Park Ridge IL 60068

Budget Films
4590 Santa Monica Blvd.
Los Angeles CA 90029

Carousel Films
1501 Broadway (Suite 1503)
New York NY 10036

Center for Mass Communications
562 W. 113th St.
New York NY 10025

Children's Film Festival
Boxoffice Bldg.
1921 Pennsylvania Ave.
Washington DC 20006

Chinese Embassy
Film Library
2311 Massachusetts Ave. NW
Washington DC 20008

Cinema Eight
Middlesex Ave.
Chester CT 06412

Cinemaesthetics
PO Box 296
New York NY 10023

Cinema 5
595 Madison Ave.
New York NY 10022

Columbia Broadcasting System
51 W. 52nd St.
New York NY 10019

Columbia Cinemateque
711 Fifth Ave.
New York NY 10022

Contemporary/McGraw-Hill Films
1221 Ave. of the Americas
New York NY 10020

Creative Film Society
7237 Canby Ave.
Reseda CA 91335

Embassy of the U.S.S.R.
Film Library
1125 16th St. NW
Washington DC 20036

Entertainment Films
c/o The Film Scene
1 Beekman Pl.
New York NY 10038

Filmaker's Library
11 Riverside Dr.
New York NY 10023

Film Classic Exchange
1926 S. Vermont Ave.
Los Angeles CA 90007

Film Images/Radim Films
17 W. 60th St.
New York NY 10023

Film-Makers' Cooperative
175 Lexington Ave.
New York NY 10016

Films for the Humanities
Harold Mantell Inc.
PO Box 378
Princeton NJ 08540

Films Incorporated
4420 Oakton St.
Skokie IL 60076

Films International
203 S. Second St.
Mankato MN 56001

Films of Israel
c/o Alden Films
5113 16th Ave.
Brooklyn NY 11204

Genesis Films
40 W. 55th St.
New York NY 10019

Grove Press Film Division
214 Mercer St.
New York NY 10012

Indiana University
Audio-Visual Center
Bloomington IN 47405

Information Service of India
975 National Press Bldg.
14th and F Sts. NW
Washington DC 20004

Instituto Italiano di Cultura
Documentary Film Service
686 Park Ave.
New York NY 10021

International Film Bureau
332 S. Michigan Ave.
Chicago IL 60604

I. Q. Films
689 Fifth Ave.
New York NY 10022

Ivy Films/16
165 W. 46th St.
New York NY 10036

Janus Films
745 Fifth Ave.
New York NY 10022

Leacock-Pennebaker
56 W. 45th St.
New York NY 10036

Lewis Film Service
1425 E. Central
Wichita KS 67214

Library of Congress
E. Capitol & Independence Ave. SE
Washington DC 20540

Macmillan Films
34 MacQuesten Pkwy. S
Mount Vernon NY 10550

Mass Media Associates
2116 N. Charles St.
Baltimore MD 21218

Maysles Films
1697 Broadway
New York NY 10019

Media International
30 E. Johnson St.
Madison WI 53703

Museum of Modern Art
Department of Film
11 W. 53rd St.
New York NY 10019

National Audio-Visual Center
Washington DC 20409

National Cinema Service
333 W. 57th St.
New York NY 10019

National Film Board of Canada
1251 Ave. of the Americas
New York NY 10020

NBC Educational Enterprises
30 Rockefeller Plaza
New York NY 10020

New Yorker Films
43 W. 61st St.
New York NY 10023

New York University
Film Library
26 Washington Pl.
New York NY 10003

Pyramid Films
PO Box 1048
Santa Monica CA 90406

Roa's Films
1696 N. Astor St.
Milwaukee WI 53202

See-Art Films
PO Box 638
Ardsley-on-Hudson NY 10503

Select Film Library
115 W. 31st St.
New York NY 10001

Silent Cinema Service
331 N. Main St.
Roxboro NC 27573

Swank Motion Pictures
201 S. Jefferson Ave.
St. Louis MO 63166

"The" Film Center
915 Twelfth St. NW
Washington DC 20005

Time-Life Multimedia
Time & Life Bldg.
New York NY 10020

Trans-World Films
322 S. Michigan Ave.
Chicago IL 60604

UNESCO
Public Information Office
Department of State
Washington DC 20502

United Artists 16
729 Seventh Ave.
New York NY 10019

United Productions of America
230 Park Ave.
New York NY 10017

University of California
Extension Media Center
2223 Fulton St.
Berkeley CA 94720

University of Illinois
Visual Aids Service
Div. of University Extension
704 S. Sixth St.
Champaign IL 61820

University of Nevada
Audio-Visual Center
Education Bldg.
Reno NV 89507

Video Tape Network
115 E. 62nd St.
New York NY 10021

Walt Disney Productions
800 Sonora Ave.
Glendale CA 91201

Walter Reade 16
241 E. 34th St.
New York NY 10016

Warner Brothers
Non-Theatrical Division
4000 Warner Blvd.
Burbank CA 91503

Welling Motion Pictures
800 Meacham Ave.
Elmont NY 11003

World Wide Pictures
1313 Hennepin Ave.
Minneapolis MN 55403

Xerox Films
245 Long Hill Rd.
Middletown CT 06457

photo credits

index

index